WORLD WAR II
IN PHOTOGRAPHS

EXECUTIVE EDITOR: Sarah Larter
ART EDITOR: Trevor Newman
DESIGN: Simon Mercer
TEXT AND PICTURE RESEARCH: Terry Charman and Neil Young
PICTURE RESEARCH: Carina Dvorak
PICTURE CO-ORDINATION: Lorna Ainger
PRODUCTION: Garry Lewis

Printed in Dubai

IMPERIAL WAR
MUSEUM

WORLD WAR II
IN PHOTOGRAPHS

RICHARD HOLMES

CARLTON

CONTENTS

INTRODUCTION

I It was a photographer's war. To be sure, photographers had captured images of earlier conflicts, starting with blurred views of the US–Mexican war of 1846–8 and going on to show Roger Fenton's hirsute warriors in the Crimea and Matthew Brady's crumpled heroes of the American Civil War. But the limitations imposed by primitive technology meant that photographers were far better at revealing war's participants or combat's aftermath – some of the most striking photographs of the Civil War show sprawled dead, boots stolen and clothes bulging horribly – than they were at recording the face of battle. The development of the dry photographic plate in the 1870s removed some technical constraints, but photographs of the Anglo–Boer War and Russo–Japanese War retain many characteristics of earlier work, with self-conscious groups clustered round artillery pieces or a trench choked with dead on Spion Kop. One of the few "combat" shots of the Boer War, showing British troops assaulting a boulder-strewn *kopje*, is almost certainly posed.

The First World War had many photographers, amateur and professional, for the development of the box camera had removed the obstacles caused by bulky equipment and unreliable technology. Yet official censorship and individual sensitivity imposed constraints of their own. At first British dead were not to be shown, and it was not until after the war that some of the most shocking images emerged. These showed dismembered bodies draping trees like macabre fruit, relics of humanity mouldering in shell-ploughed earth or – sometimes more shocking to humans who can accommodate the sufferings of their own race but are touched by the plight of animals – dead horses tumbled where shrapnel had caught their gun-team. The war went a step further, with the 1916 production *The Battle of the Somme* breaking new ground by showing cinema audiences film (part staged and part actuality) of a battle in progress.

Although there is abundant film of the Second World War, somehow it is the photograph that freezes the moment for posterity. The war is defined by its icons – like St Paul's Cathedral standing triumphant amid the smoke of the London Blitz; MacArthur wading through Philippine surf as he made good his promise to return, and the raising of the US flag on Mount Suribachi on the Pacific island of Iwo Jima. These icons are, all too often, false. MacArthur and his entourage waded ashore a second time when it photographers missed their first landing, and the flag-raising on Iwo Jima was a repeat, for the camera, of an

earlier, less flamboyant act. Yet recognition of the fact that the camera often lies scarcely dents our desire to believe what we see.

The great majority of the photographs in this book come from the archives of London's Imperial War Museum. The museum is the repository for official British photographs of the Second World War, and includes shots from a dozen theatres of war, taken by a variety of photographers. Many served with the Army Film and Photographic Unit: some were destined to remain unknown, while others, like Cecil Beaton, were already acknowledged as masters of their craft. Others were officers and men who broke the rules to freeze the moment in Brownie of Kodak. Sometimes an annotation on the print reflects the risks they ran: the original caption to one photograph (p.222) notes that the photographer had already been sunk that day but had managed to keep his camera dry and worked on aboard the ship that rescued him. And sometimes the photograph itself makes it all too clear that the man who took it was at the very sharpest end of war.

The Museum also holds photographs taken by Allied photographers, among them Robert Capa, whose coverage of the Spanish Civil War had already made him famous. He accompanied American forces in Italy, and landed with them in Normandy: his views of *Omaha* beach triggered the initial sequence in Steven Spielberg's film *Saving Private Ryan*. Among the Red Army's photographers was the excellent Yevgeniy Khaldei, who took the series atop the ruined Reichstag in 1945. In addition to captured German and Japanese official photographs there are several sets of privately taken German photographs that throw new light on the war. One of Hitler's personal staff took some intimate shots of the Führer and his entourage in 1938–9; Rommel's album includes some personal shots of the 1940 campaign, and Field Marshal Wolfram von Richthofen, a German air force commander in Italy, had his own wartime album.

This has been a collaborative venture from start to finish. At its start I met the research team, Carina Dvorak, Terry Charman, Nigel Steel and Neil Young, with Sarah Larter of Carlton Books keeping us on track, to discuss the book's outline and establish the topics which photographs were to cover. We tried, on the one hand, not to weigh the book too heavily towards the Anglo–American view of the war nor, on the other, to make it so eclectic that the conflict's main thrusts were obscured. While most of the images are indeed war photographs, many are not, and reflect the fact that this war – arguably the greatest event in world history – affected millions of people who neither wore uniform nor shouldered a weapon. The researchers then ransacked their resources and emerged with a short list of shots from which, in another series of meetings, we made the final selection. The short list was always rather a long one, and at the end of the process I was easily persuaded that we had enough photographs for a book on each year of the war.

The selection includes many of the war's classic shots (such as MacArthur in the Philippines and the flag-raisers on Iwo Jima) as well as dozens which are far less well known, and some which have not previously been published. Some areas are well covered and others are not: for instance, there are few worthwhile photographs of the Allied campaign against the Vichy French garrison of the Levant in 1941. We tried to include as many combat shots as we could, although this was not always easy: it is often clear, either from the photograph itself or its context in a collection, that many alleged combat photographs are in fact posed. Sometimes the photographer's own position is the give-away: mistrust sharp shots of infantry advancing, with steely determination, on the photographer, and shots of anti-tank guns or artillery pieces taken from the weapon's front. We tried to avoid formal portraits, preferring, where we could, to catch the war's main actors in unguarded moments.

I wrote all the captions, generally relying on the original for guidance, although it was evident that some captions, often for reasons of wartime security, were economical with the truth while others were plainly misleading. Sometimes I was assisted by evidence which has recently come to light. In one poignant case (p.351) the daughter of a policeman consoling an old man sitting on the wreckage of his ruined home identified her father in the shot that typified him as the "good and caring man" that his family remembered him as. There will be cases – although, I hope, not too many of them – when I will have compounded an error made by the original caption (or, indeed, introduced one of my own), just as there will be times when a posed photograph has hoodwinked my team and me.

The book is organized by year, which has the merit of giving a sense of pace and coherence which the reader should find helpful. It must be acknowledged, though, that an annuality which helps historians and their readers was often not apparent to the war's participants, and many campaigns – like the British *Compass* offensive in the Western Desert in 1940–1 did not pause for Christmas. Although *Picture Post*, which published Capa's photographs of the Spanish Civil War, maintained that they were "simply a record of modern war from the inside", I do not believe that photographs can stand alone. Accordingly, I have prefaced each year with an account of its major events, and provided each block of photographs within it with a brief introduction. Although I hope that the photographs reflect the war's near universality, there will be times when the text cannot do so without being repetitive. But I warmly acknowledge that most of the "British" armies I describe included substantial contingents from self-governing dominions which supported the alliance as a matter of choice. No Englishman of my father's generation could fail to acknowledge the contribution made by Australia, Canada and New Zealand, by African troops in North Africa and Burma, or to applaud the British–Indian Army, emerging triumphant from the last of its many wars. Neither would he forget that in the great Allied onslaught of 1944 Belgians, Czechs, Free Frenchmen, Norwegians and Poles were among those who risked their lives in the cause of freedom.

This leads me to my final point. Some of my fellow historians believe that the Second World War was a conflict from which Britain could have stepped aside: that it was in her best interests to seek an accommodation with Hitler in 1940. I do not share this view. It is beyond question that the war was strewn with moral complexities. On the Axis side, many good men fought bravely in a bad cause from which, even if they wished, they had little real chance of dissenting. Although recent research persuades me that military recognition of Nazism's darker side was wider than the German armed forces' many Anglo–American admirers once admitted, it required an extraordinary moral courage (for which members of the German Resistance merit our applause) to confront the corporate state's ideological juggernaut. I am not sure that I would have had that courage, especially if the lives of my family depended on my stance.

The strategic bombing of Germany and Japan raises issues of its own, and it is infinitely easier to strike a moral stance with the clear vision of hindsight than it was at the time, when bitterness, desire for revenge and a wish to preserve friendly lives blurred the sight. Stalin, who appears, smiling benevolently, in this book, had little to learn from Hitler as far as mass murder was concerned, and his own security apparatus (as photographs of the Katyn massacre demonstrate) was as ugly as that of Nazi Germany. Yet the Red Army included a mass of decent folk for whom the conflict was indeed the Great Patriotic War. On the other hand the fate of members of minorities who fought for the Germans – the Cossacks are a classic case in point – may, rightly, move us. So there are few simplicities and abundant contradictions. Yet ultimately this was a war in which good was pitted against evil: and if the world which emerged from it brought tensions and tragedies of its own, surely we have only to consider the implications of an Axis victory to recognize the magnitude of the Allied triumph. That, ultimately, is the story of this book.

RICHARD HOLMES

1 9 3 9

THE OUTBREAK OF WAR

THE SECOND WORLD WAR WAS THE BLOODIEST CONFLICT IN HISTORY. EVEN NOW WE CANNOT BE SURE OF ITS REAL HUMAN COST. THE LOSSES OF THE WESTERN ALLIES WERE SUBSTANTIAL: THE BRITISH ARMED FORCES HAD 264,000 KILLED (ROUGHLY THE SAME AS UNITED STATES MILITARY DEAD) THE MERCHANT NAVY LOST 30,248 MEN AND 60,500 BRITISH CIVILIANS WERE KILLED BY BOMBING.

GERMAN LOSSES were higher: some two million service personnel were killed and almost as many reported missing, while up to a million civilians perished in air attacks. Further east, numbers are not only much higher but accurate figures are harder to obtain. China lost perhaps five million military dead, with another ten to twenty million civilian dead. Japanese dead, civilian and military, exceeded two million, and such was the impact of American bombing that by the end of the war an estimated 8.5 million Japanese were homeless. Perhaps ten million Russian servicemen perished, and one estimate puts Russia's real demographic loss – including children unborn – at a staggering 48 million.

These figures reflect an astonishing diversity of sacrifice. A single firestorm in Tokyo on March 9–10, 1945, killed almost 85,000 civilians; between 1.2 and 1.5 million victims died in Auschwitz; one estimate puts dead in the Soviet Gulag at a million a year; 13,500 Russians were executed by other Russians at Stalingrad; almost 6,000 US Marines died taking the Pacific island of Iwo Jima, and when the German liner *Wilhelm Gustloff* was torpedoed by a Soviet submarine in the Baltic on January 30, 1945, perhaps 6,000 troops and civilians went to the bottom with her in the largest single loss of life in maritime history. Yet sheer numbers somehow veil the reality of suffering, and it is human stories on a smaller scale that the really make the point. We identify with the fourteen-year-old Anne Frank, trembling in her garret in Amsterdam; with a London air-raid warden's report of an untouched meal in an intact house while the family of six who were to eat it were "scattered over a large area" after a bomb, perversely,

struck their air-raid shelter; or with Pacific War veteran and writer William Manchester's recollection of shooting "a robin-fat, moon-faced roly-poly little man" whose killing left him "a thing of tears and twitchings and dirtied pants."

It was a total war, the tools of which included snipers' rifles and super-heavy artillery, midget submarines and aircraft carriers, single-seat fighters and strategic bombers, delivering death and wounds, war's old currency, though bullet, high explosive, liquid fire and, latterly, the atomic bomb. It transformed national economies and the lives of countless millions. Its shadow fell across the whole globe. The Australian city of Darwin was bombed by Japanese aircraft and the German-occupied Lofoten Islands of Norway were raided by British commandos. Moroccan cavalrymen died fighting German tanks in northern France, Indians killed Germans in North Africa, Australians perished in Malayan jungles, Cossacks died under Allied bombs in Normandy, and Japanese–Americans fought with distinction in Italy. It was, as the historian M.R.D. Foot has brilliantly put it, not so much two-sided as polygonal, with both the broad war-fighting coalitions, the Allies and the Axis, subsuming ideological and cultural differences that sometimes emerged even when the war was in progress and appeared, with depressing clarity, after its conclusion.

Its causes were complex, and although its outbreak (like that of so many wars) might have been averted by greater political wisdom or more moral courage, it was not, unlike the First World War, brought about by last-minute miscalculation. The mainsprings of conflict were coiled deep into the nineteenth-century. Germany's victory over France in the Franco–Prussian War of 1870–71 left France embittered, Germany militaristic and Europe unbalanced. In one sense the Franco–Prussian War was the beginning of a European civil war that lasted, with long armistices, until the end of the Cold War in the last decade of the Twentieth Century. It helped establish the conditions that enabled war to come so easily in 1914: the acutely time-sensitive railway-borne mobilization of mass armies composed of young men brought up to believe that dying for one's country was sweet and seemly; military technology that had enhanced killing power but done far less for the ability to communicate; and the widely shared belief in the inevitability of a great struggle which, on the one hand, would justify a nation's right to exist and, on the other, would test the manhood of participants.

There is no doubt that the Second World War flared up from the ashes of the First. The connection is most apparent in the case of Germany, where resentment at the Treaty of Versailles (the separation of East Prussia from the rest of Germany by the "Polish corridor" was particularly hated), discontent with the politics of the Weimar republic and vulnerability to the economic pressures of the 1920s fanned a desire for change which Hitler was able to exploit. He came to power in 1933, repudiated the Versailles settlement two years later, and when he reintroduced conscription in 1935, the 100,000-man Reichswehr, the army allowed Germany by Versailles, formed the nucleus for military expansion. Armoured warfare theorists, Guderian chief among them, had paid careful attention to developments in Britain and France, and had ideas of their own. It is simplistic to contrast innovative and forward-looking Germans with narrow-minded conservatives in Britain and France, for Germany too had its reactionaries and there were radical thinkers in the British and French armed forces; it is true to say that Germany began to develop cohesive tactical doctrine based on the combined use of armour and air power while the western Allies did not.

America, whose President Wilson had played such a key role in forming the terms of the Versailles Treaty, withdrew from a Europe whose new, fragile internal frontiers she had done much to shape. Her failure to join the League of Nations was one of the reasons why that body never attained the influence hoped for by its founders. Yet without security guarantees many of the shoots planted by Versailles were tender indeed. Czechoslovakia had a minority population of Sudeten Germans, and little real cultural integrity, while Poland included elements of former German and Russian territory, reminding the Germans of Versailles and the Russians of their 1920 defeat before Warsaw in the Russo–Polish war. Yugoslavia – "Land of the South Slavs" – was a fragile bonding of disparate elements: just how fragile we were to see in the 1990s.

Britain and France, for their part, hoped that they had indeed just witnessed "the war to end war." Both faced political and economic challenges, and showed little real desire to police at Versailles settlement, in part because of the cost of maintaining armed forces capable of doing so, and in part because some of their political leaders applauded Hitler's stand against the "Bolshevik menace" and believed that Germany had been treated too harshly by Versailles. Moreover, French and British statesmen of the 1930s had the evidence of 1914 behind them, and it was all too easy for them, in striving to avoid repeating the rush to war of July 1914, to appease a dictator whose appetite was in fact insatiable. In consequence, Germany's 1936 reoccupation of the Rhineland went unopposed. After the Anschluss, Germany's union with Austria in March 1938, Czechoslovakia was Hitler's next target, and at Munich in September 1938 the British and French premiers agreed to the German dismemberment of that unfortunate state. Historical opinion on Munich remains divided: some historians argue that France and Britain should have gone to war then, while others maintain that the agreement bought them a year's respite in which to rearm.

Italy, whose entry into the First World War had been heavily influenced by the lure of reward, felt poorly compensated by the peace settlement for the hammering taken by her army. Benito Mussolini's fascist regime, which came to power in 1922, rejoiced in the opportunity to take a forward foreign policy, in the face of League of Nations condemnation, by overrunning Abyssinia in 1935–36. International ostracism pushed Italy closer to Germany, and there was in any case a natural convergence between Italian Fascism and German Nazism. In October 1936 the Rome–Berlin

Axis was formed, and in May 1939 Hitler and Mussolini signed the "Pact of Steel." Both sent men to fight for the Nationalists during the Spanish Civil War, and the Germans in particular learnt useful lessons there: one of their generals, comparing it to one of the British army's training-grounds, called it "the European Aldershot."

Japan was also a dissatisfied victor, and she too suffered from the recessions of the 1920s. The growing part played by her aggressive but disunited military in successive governments generated instability, her dissatisfaction with the outcome of the London naval conference of 1930, which agreed quota for warship construction, created further pressures, and in 1936 her delegates withdrew from the second London conference, leaving Japan free to build warships without restriction from 1937. Friction between army and navy over the defence budget led to an uneasy compromise. The army, which invaded Manchuria in 1931, at the cost of Japan's membership of the League of Nations, pushed on into China itself. This brought the risk of confrontation with the Soviet Union, and in August 1939 the Japanese were badly beaten by the Russians at Khalkin-Gol. The navy, meanwhile, took the first steps of southwards expansion into the "Greater East Asian co-prosperity sphere," taking Hainan Island and the Spratly Islands in 1939.

Although Russian sources consistently refer to the Second World War as the "Great Patriotic War," Russia was engaged in expansion long before the German–Soviet war broke out. However, her armed forces suffered from an ideological insistence on the centrality of the masses, which impeded the full development of some far-sighted military doctrine pioneered by Marshal Tukhachevsky and his associates. They were then badly disrupted by Stalin's purges of 1937–38, which deprived the forces of about 35,000 of an officer corps of some 80,000. In November 1939 Russia attacked Finland, which had gained her independence in 1917, and the ensuing campaign showed the Red Army in a poor light. Zhukov's defeat of the Japanese at Khalkin-Gol that August had, though, given an early indication of the Red Army's enormous potential. In the same month German foreign minister Ribbentrop and People's Commissar for Foreign Affairs Molotov signed a pact that left the way clear for the division of Poland after the Germans attacked the following month.

The German invasion of Poland made it clear that appeasement had failed, and left France and Britain, their bluff called, with no alternative to declaring war on Germany. There was little that they could do for the unlucky Poles, whose brave but old-fashioned army was first lacerated by German armour and air power and then, on September 17, stabbed in the back by the Russians. The French, scarred by their experience of the First World War which had left one-third of Frenchmen under thirty dead or crippled and a strip of murdered nature across the north, had ploughed a huge investment into the steel and concrete of the Maginot Line, which covered sections of the Franco–German border. It stopped short at the Belgian border, and when Belgium, hitherto a French ally, declared her neutrality in 1936, there was no money available to continue it along the northern frontier in any serious way. Although some French officers, among them a lanky colonel called Charles de Gaulle, took armoured warfare seriously, in all too many respects the French army of 1939 closely resembled that of 1918.

Britain, too, had its apostles of armoured war, like Basil Liddell Hart and Major General J. F. C. Fuller, but although the army had embraced mechanization, and had almost entirely removed the horse from its inventory by 1939, its experiments with tanks, once so promising, had not come to full fruition. As late as December 1937 the dispatch of an expeditionary force to support a European ally was accorded the lowest priority, below the maintenance of colonial commitments and the defence of the United Kingdom against air attack. In the latter context, though, the time bought at Munich had been put to good use, for work on a new fighter, the Spitfire, and on Radio Detecting And Ranging (RADAR) was completed in time to allow both to play a full part in 1940.

The fact remained that the allies could do nothing to help the Poles, and as British and French soldiers spent the winter of 1939–40, the worst for years, in their freezing positions on the frontier, it is small wonder that they gave the war unflattering nicknames. To the French it was the *drôle de guerre*, and to the British "the phoney war", a term coined by US Senator Borah. Some even made a pun on the new word *blitzkrieg* – lightning war – coined by a journalist to describe the German attack on Poland: they called it *sitzkrieg*.

THE RISE OF HITLER

The origins of the Second World War were rooted in the First. German resentment at the Versailles Treaty, economic crisis, nationalism, militarism and anti-Semitism all helped bring the Nazis to power. Hitler was appointed chancellor of Germany by President Hindenburg in January 1933. It was after the burning of the Reichstag, which he blamed on Bolsheviks and other anti-social elements, and elections on March 5, which the Nazi Party and its nationalist allies won, that Hitler strengthened his grip. On the Night of the Long Knives, June 30, 1934, Hitler purged the party and when Hindenburg died, he combined the offices of President and Chancellor in himself as Führer. Germany became a centralized state ruled by one party.

BELOW
On "Kristallnacht", November 9–10, 1938, thousands of Jewish properties were attacked: these are the ruins of a Berlin synagogue.

OPPOSITE PAGE
Fireman work on the burning shell of the German parliament building, the Reichstag, February 27, 1933.

Nazi Party rallies, such as this one in
Nuremberg in 1935, were emotive displays
of group solidarity that also indicated to the
world the full strength of Hitler's power.

RIGHT
The Rhineland was demilitarized by
the Treaty of Versailles, but in March 1936
the German army moved in, to the
evident delight of the inhabitants.

THE ITALIAN INVASION OF ABYSSINIA

The ancient East African kingdom of Abyssinia had humiliatingly defeated an Italian invasion in 1896, which the Italians sought to avenge in October 1935. This time they invaded from their adjacent territories of Italian Somaliland and Eritrea and, deploying the full panoply of modern war, decisively defeated the Abyssinians in 1936. This image shows Italian troops advancing into Abyssinia.

THE SPANISH CIVIL WAR

The violent unrest that followed the election of the Popular Front government in Spain led, in July 1936, to a military coup led by General Franco. Civil War followed, with traditionalist and fascist Nationalists fighting an even broader left-wing coalition of Republicans. The war mirrored wider political divisions outside Spain. Substantial German, Italian and Portuguese contingents were among the "volunteers" who fought for the Nationalists, while an assortment of foreigners, including a small Russian contingent, supported the Republicans. The war was characterized – as civil wars so often are – by great brutality, and was won by the Nationalists, supported by Hitler and Mussolini, in 1939.

RIGHT
Patchily equipped Republican militiamen with a local girl near Aragon, 1936.

BELOW
Tanks of the German *Kondor Legion* in action in Spain.

Increasing numbers of Republican refugees
trudged to the French frontier in early 1939.

THE SINO–JAPANESE CONFLICT

In 1931 Japan invaded the Chinese province of Manchuria, which was proclaimed the puppet state of Manchukuo the following year, and in 1937 the Japanese launched a full-scale invasion of China. The fighting gave a grim foretaste of what was to come elsewhere, with towns bombed and civilians becoming involved in an ugly war.

LEFT

Volunteer members of the Chunking fire brigade fighting fires caused by Japanese bombing.

BELOW

Japanese soldiers march through a Chinese town.

THE ADVENT OF WAR

The Italian fascist leader Benito Mussolini came to power in 1922 and became dictator three years later. In October 1936, Hitler and Mussolini formed the Berlin–Rome axis, and next month Germany and Japan concluded the Anti-Comintern pact. Hitler outlined his programme to his service chiefs in November 1937, and set about the territorial expansion that led to war. In March 1938, Austria was annexed, and in September, the Munich Agreement enabled Germany to annex the Sudeten district of Czechoslovakia. Bohemia-Moravia was made into a German protectorate in March 1939, Lithuania ceded Memel to Germany in the same month, and on September 1, 1939, Germany invaded Poland.

ABOVE
Mussolini attended the Wehrmacht's 1937 manoeuvres. The substantial figure of Hermann Göring is half-hidden between him and Hitler and Hans Frank, later Governor-General of Poland, is on Mussolini's immediate right. On Frank's right Colonel General von Fritsch, chief of the general staff (who was dismissed the following year after a false accusation of impropriety) is chatting to Lt General Wilhelm Keitel, who was later to run the Armed Forces High Command, Oberkommando der Wehrmacht.

LEFT

Signs of the times. On March 12, 1938, a Viennese square named for the Austrian Chancellor, Engelbert Dollfuss, murdered during an attempted Nazi coup in 1934, receives its new name.

BELOW

British Prime Minister Neville Chamberlain arriving at Heston airport after the Munich conference in September 1938, he was later to declare infamously "Peace in Our Time".

LEFT
Nazi policies unleashed a flood of
Jewish refugees, although not all
were as fortunate as Renate Lewy, an
11-year-old who found asylum in Britain.

BELOW
Czech President Emil Hacha, hopelessly
isolated by the Munich Agreement and
visibly close to the collapse which required
the attention of Hitler's doctor, Theodor
Morell, about to sign away his state.

German Mk II tanks in Wenceslas
Square, Prague, April 20, 1939.

ABOVE
German sailors march into Memel, March 23, 1939.

ABOVE
This informal photograph by Nicolaus von Below, Hitler's Luftwaffe adjutant, shows Hitler, Göring, Keitel and foreign minister, Joachim von Ribbentrop lunching on August 22, 1939 at the Berghof, Hitler's retreat above Berchtesgaden in the Bavarian Alps. They have been finalizing the strategy for the invasion of Poland, which was just over a week away.

THE INVASION OF POLAND
AND THE DECLARATION OF WAR

In August 1939, the Ribbentrop–Molotov pact was signed by the foreign ministers of Germany and Russia. It was the last step in the isolation of Poland, upon whom both Russia and Germany had designs, and at dawn on September 1, the German invasion began. Polish courage and outdated equipment were no match for the Wehrmacht, using its blitzkrieg tactics for the first time. The Russians attacked on September 17, and organized Polish resistance ended on October 5. The German invasion of Poland was the last straw for Britain and France, who declared war on September 3.

OPPOSITE PAGE
The faces say it all. French Premier Edouard Daladier (second from right) and his cabinet return from the Elysée Palace on September 2, 1939 having agreed to order general mobilization. Jean Zay, education minister, manages a brave smile.

BELOW
The French had built fortifications along their border with Germany to protect themselves from invasion. Known as the Maginot Line, they were to prove ineffective, largely because they persuaded the Germans to attack elsewhere.

ABOVE
Newspaper placards announce the German
invasion of Poland, September 1, 1939.

LEFT
A War Emergency Reserve policeman joins a more traditionally dressed colleague outside Number 10 Downing Street.

RIGHT
The first (false) air-raid warnings followed the declaration of war. Here, a policeman blowing his whistle to draw attention to his warning sign, cycles down Whitehall, September 3, 1939. The milkman behind him seems set on business as usual.

LEFT
Winston Churchill was appointed First Lord of the Admiralty on the outbreak of war. He held the same appointment in August 1914, and on hearing the news the Admiralty Board signalled to the fleet: "Winston is back". This unposed photograph shows Churchill arriving at work, complete with dispatch boxes and bundle of office keys.

RIGHT
British Prime Minister, Neville Chamberlain, and his war cabinet.

ABOVE
Rites of passage and, all too
probably, the final meeting: a Polish
woman slips something into her husband's
knapsack as he leaves for the front.

A German reconnaissance
unit in Poland, September 1939.

Early on September 1, 1939, the old
German training battleship, *Schleswig-
Holstein*, on a "goodwill" visit to Danzig,
opened fire on the Polish-held enclave of
Westerplatte. The Poles held out bravely
before surrendering on September 7.

Hitler made several trips to the Polish front in September 1939. Here he receives the salute of General der Panzertruppen Heinz Guderian, one of the authors of the blitzkrieg that made German victory possible.

The best of friends? Russian and German officers chat at Brest-Litovsk on September 18, 1939. The Russians show their rank on collar badges: the traditional epaulettes, hated symbol of the tsarist officer class, were to appear after the German invasion. The black-uniformed German is a panzer officer.

LEFT
The remnants of the garrison of Warsaw, marching out of the city after its surrender, September 27, 1939. Most of the buildings show the damage inflicted by German bombardments and air-raids.

RIGHT
Poland had a large Jewish population, and the invading Germans rapidly set about rounding it up: an aged Jew is detained in Warsaw.

LEFT
German propaganda minister Joseph Goebbels had Warsaw plastered with posters showing a wounded Polish soldier pointing to the city's ruins and saying "England! This is your work!" The Poles were unconvinced and in November 1939, two women were executed for tearing down a poster.

THE PHONEY WAR

During the so-called phoney war, between September 1939 and April 1940, unemployment in Britain remained high, mobilization seemed sluggish, and there was little major war news. However, there was widespread fear of air attack, in which poison gas might be used, and the fact that the nation was indeed at war was underlined by air raid precautions and the evacuation of children from larger cities. In September, over 800,000 unaccompanied children and more than 500,000 mothers with young children left the cities, although as the expected attack failed to materialize eighty percent had returned home by the beginning of 1940.

BELOW
Families filling sandbags at Bognor Regis on August 30. The original print bears the caption: "A New Beach Pastime".

OPPOSITE PAGE
A nurse demonstrates the
gas mask issued for babies.

LEFT
Schoolchildren from North London –
prominently labelled for identification –
leaving the railway station on arrival
at their provincial destination.

BELOW
Popular entertainment helped maintain
morale. Here RAF men are doing the
"Lambeth Walk" with Lupino Lane and
the cast of the hit musical *Me and My Girl*.

FRANCE PREPARES

France planned to fight a long war, with the Maginot Line safeguarding her from German attack while her war machine gradually built up speed. The French army was a mixture of ancient and modern, with infantry and artillery reminiscent of 1918 and, although it had some good tanks, too many of these were allocated to infantry support. Lord Gort's British Expeditionary Force (BEF) went to France in 1939 and established its headquarters at Arras, in the midst of World War One battlefields remembered by many of its members.

ABOVE
French infantry on the march, September 1939.

RIGHT
French tanks on manoeuvres, autumn 1939.
When the Germans invaded on 10 May 1940, France could field 2,285 tanks on her north-eastern front.

RIGHT

RIGHT

In September 1939, the French army launched a cautious offensive in the Saar. It did at least provide evidence, like this photograph taken privately by a French officer, that some German territory had been occupied.

BELOW

French gunners with a 75 mm field-gun. The weapon, the workhorse of the French army in the First World War, was now past its best.

LEFT
Leading elements of the BEF
arrive in France, September 1939.

BELOW
Although the censor has blacked out
details that might give a clue to the
location of these railway wagons, there
are the same "40 men-8 horses" wagons
familiar to British soldiers of an
earlier war, on the way to the British
concentration area around Arras.

LEFT

This photograph of Lord Gort (centre) with War Minister Leslie Hore-Belisha gives no clue that the two got on badly: the energetic but sharp tongued Hore-Belisha was forced to resign soon after this picture was taken. The only officer in battledress is Major General Bernard Montgomery, commanding Gort's 3rd Division.

BELOW

Neville Chamberlain enjoys a cup of coffee and a biscuit after flying to France to visit the BEF and its air component.

THE BATTLE OF THE RIVER PLATE

The German pocket battleship *Graf Spee* had left port with her supply ship *Altmark* before war broke out. She sank nine merchant ships before steaming back to Germany for repairs. On the way her captain, Hans Langsdorff, headed for the River Plate to intercept a convoy, but was met by Commodore Henry Harwood's Force G with the light cruisers *Ajax* and *Achilles* and the larger *Exeter*. Although the British warships were damaged, Langsdorff was forced to put into Montevideo in neutral Uruguay. Compelled to leave, he scuttled his ship and later committed suicide. The battle gave a fillip to British morale.

PREVIOUS PAGES
The *Graf Spee* scuttled on the orders of her captain, in flames in the River Plate off Montevideo.

ABOVE
Some of *Graf Spee*'s crew watch as the British steamer *Trevanion* is sunk.

THE RUSSIAN INVASION OF FINLAND

When Russia invaded Finland on November 30 1939, the Finns fought back hard. Well-trained ski troops, nicknamed "White Death" inflicted enormous casualties on the Russians, but eventually, weight of numbers and machinery told: in February 1940, the Russians breached the Mannerheim Line between Lake Lagoda and the Gulf of Finland, forcing the Finns to come to terms on March 12, 1940. The image here shows Finnish ski troops passing through a small town, December 20, 1939.

1940
BRITAIN STANDS ALONE

IN 1940 THE SMOULDERING WAR BURST INTO FLAME. THE FIRST FLICKERS CAME IN THE NORTH. AS EARLY AS SEPTEMBER 1939 CHURCHILL, FIRST LORD OF THE ADMIRALTY, PLANNED TO LAY MINES IN THE LEADS, THE SHIPPING CHANNEL ALONG THE NORWEGIAN COAST, WHILE FRENCH PREMIER EDOUARD DALADIER HOPED FOR "SUCCESSFUL NAVAL ACTION IN THE BALTIC." PAUL REYNAUD, WHO REPLACED HIM IN MARCH 1940, WAS EQUALLY SUPPORTIVE OF ALLIED INTERVENTION IN NORWAY.

THE GERMANS, for their part, scented the possibility of acquiring naval bases on the Norwegian coast. Finland's brave resistance against the Russians encouraged the Allies to toy with a scheme for landing at Narvik, in north Norway, crossing into Sweden, securing the ore-fields on the north, and going on to aid the Finns. Not only would this have violated both Norwegian and Swedish neutrality but, as the British historian T.K. Derry has observed, "the pattern of alliances would have been transformed."

Finland's capitulation put an end to this scheme, but not to other projects. Norwegian territorial waters were entered by British and German vessels, and in February 1940 sailors from HMS *Cossack* boarded *Altmark*, supply ship of the pocket battleship *Graf Spee*, scuttled the previous year, and liberated prisoners taken from *Graf Spee*'s victims. The act helped persuade the Germans that the Allies were close to an attack on Norway which the Norwegians (who had not fired on *Cossack*) would not resist. The Allies, on the other hand, believed that the Norwegians felt unable to check German use of their sea-lanes.

Both sides decided to act. The Allies began to mine the Leads, expecting that this would provoke the Germans and justify an Allied response. The Germans, however, launched Operation *Weserübung*, a full-scale invasion of Norway and Denmark. Although the British got wind of it, they proved unable to intercept seaborne invasion forces, and by nightfall on April 9, the Germans had seized Oslo,

Bergen, Trondheim and Narvik, using airborne troops to seize Oslo airport. They suffered loss in doing so: for instance, an ancient shore battery covering Oslo sunk the modern cruiser *Blücher*. And the Norwegians fought back, despite the efforts of the pro-German Vidkun Quisling, whose name was to be taken into the English language as a synonym for collaborator.

Despite their expectation that the Germans would indeed strike, the scale and speed of their enterprise caught the Allies flat-footed. The Allies made landings at various points along the coast, but in most cases the troops involved were poorly prepared for the venture and all but helpless in the face of German air power. Only at Narvik was there a glimmer of success. There the ten destroyers that had transported a mountain division to the port were attacked and, in two separate battles, all sunk or driven ashore. An Allied force, which included Polish as well as British and French troops, captured Narvik on May 28. But by this time, as we shall see, events elsewhere had turned against the Allies, and Narvik had to be evacuated, an event marred by the loss of the aircraft carrier *Glorious*.

The Norwegian campaign, mishandled as it was by the Allies, had three outcomes which were to redound to their advantage. The first was that the Germans were compelled to retain a substantial force in Norway throughout the war, contributing to their strategic overstretch. The second was that the campaign finished Neville Chamberlain, whose comment, just before the campaign, that Hitler had "missed the bus" was especially unfortunate. He was replaced by Churchill, whose colossal energy, which sometimes burst out as interference in the detailed conduct of military affairs, helped transform Britain's war effort, stiffen popular resolve to fight on, and, not least, to strengthen Britain's relationship with the United States. The third was the acquisition of the Norwegian Merchant Marine (the world's third largest merchant fleet) for the Allied cause.

The Norwegian campaign served as a matador's cloak for a far more serious German offensive. Hitler's rapid victory over Poland in 1939 had caught his planners ill-prepared for an attack on France and the Low Countries, and their first schemes for invasion were unenterprising. An attack across the Franco–German border was clearly ill-advised in view of the fact that the Maginot Line covered its important sectors. Instead, German planners proposed to swing widely through Holland and Belgium in an operation that resembled the Schlieffen Plan of 1914. This did not appeal to some of those involved, notably Lieutenant General Erich von Manstein, Chief of Staff to Colonel General von Rundstedt's Army Group A. Manstein developed a plan intended, as he put it, "to force a decisive issue by land". It assigned a purely defensive role to Army Group C, covering the Maginot Line, while Army Group B, in the north, would move into Holland and Belgium. But the decisive blow would be struck by Army Group A, which would contain the bulk of Germany's panzer divisions, and would use them to break through the French line in the Meuse, just south of the hilly Ardennes, and would then drive hard for the Channel coast, cutting the Allied armies in half. The plan horrified some senior officers, one of whom warned that: "You are cramming a mass of tanks together in the narrow roads of the Ardennes as if there was no such thing as air power." However, Hitler approved of it, arguing that the morale of the French army had been undermined by the vagaries of prewar politics: it would not withstand a single massive blow.

The Allies had intelligence of initial German plans, whose security was in any case compromised when a courier carrying a copy landed, by mistake, in Belgium. Their left wing, including the BEF and the best mobile elements in the French army, were to move into Belgium once here neutrality was violated, taking up a position east of Brussels to block the German advance. Both sides were numerically evenly matched with 136 divisions, although in the Allied case this included 22 Belgian and 10 Dutch divisions which would not be committed until after the Germans had attacked. The Allies had slightly more tanks than the Germans, and some of them – like the French B1 heavy tank and Somua S65 – were by no means contemptible. But the Germans not only enjoyed a clear lead in the air, but grouped their tanks, with mechanized infantry (panzer grenadiers) in cohesive panzer divisions. They had the experience of Poland behind them, and the rise in Germany's fortunes in the late 1930s had helped boost morale.

When the German offensive began on May 10, the Allied left wing rolled forward, as planned, into Belgium. The Germans staged several *coups de main* – the huge Belgian fortress of Eben Emael was taken by glider troops who landed on top of it – while their armoured spearhead entered the "impenetrable" Ardennes. It was bravely but ineffectually opposed by Belgian and French troops, and reached the Meuse on May 12: an enterprising major general called Erwin Rommel even got his advance guard across the river that day. Guderian's panzer corps crossed in strength at Sedan the next day, and speedily pushed on across France. The French commander-in-chief, General Maurice Gamelin, in his headquarters at Vincennes, on the eastern edge of Paris, was consistently wrong-footed. Although the German high command was far from perfect – Guderian had a stand-up row with his superior, Kleist – German tanks reached the Channel coast near Abbeville on May 20.

The German breakthrough left the BEF, Belgian army and part of the French army encircled in the north. The Belgians, who actually fought harder than most Anglo-French historians give them credit for – surrendered on May 28. By this time Lord Gort, the BEF's commander had taken the courageous decision to evacuate the BEF through the port of Dunkirk. Although more than one-third of the troops evacuated were French, the incident soured Anglo-French relations.

Dunkirk did not end the campaign. The newly-appointed French Commander-in-Chief, General Maxime Weygand, had done his unavailing best to cobble together a counterattack into the flanks of the panzer corridor, and now, as the Germans swung south for the second phase of the campaign. There was heavy fighting on the Somme, and the French 4th Armoured Division under de Gaulle launched a vigorous counterattack near Abbeville in late May, though it lacked the weight to do serious damage. 7th Panzer Division, under Rommel, marked out by his success during the campaign as one of the German Army's rising stars, snatched a crossing over the Somme on June 5, badly denting French confidence. Nevertheless, French troops fought on, sometimes with the courage of desperation: the cavalry cadets at Saumur held the crossings of the Loire for two days against superior forces. And, despite Dunkirk, there were still British troops engaged. The 51st Highland Division made a fighting retreat to the coast, and was eventually forced to surrender at St Valéry-en-Caux on June 12, and other British and Canadian troops were evacuated from Normandy after a dispiriting campaign. The Germans entered Paris on June 14. Marshal Petain, the aged hero of the First World War battle of Verdun, took over as premier, and an armistice was signed on the June 22 – in the same railway carriage in which the 1918 armistice had been concluded.

France was now out of the war and divided between Occupied and Unoccupied Zones. Its government, the *Etat Français,* which replaced the Third Republic, was established in the little spa town of Vichy. Not all Frenchmen were prepared to accept the verdict of 1940. Charles de Gaulle, an acting brigadier general and, briefly, member of the Reynaud government, flew to England, denounced the armistice, telling his countrymen that France had lost the battle but not the war, and set up a provisional national committee which the British speedily recognized. However, the creation of Free France left hard questions unanswered. The British were concerned that the Germans would lay hands on the powerful French fleet, and were unaware of the fact that Petain's navy minister, Admiral Darlan, had made it clear to his captains that this never to occur. On July 3, after unsatisfactory negotiations, a French squadron at anchor at Mers-el-Kebir was bombarded by a British force under Admiral Somerville. The episode, rendered all the more painful by the fact that Britain and

France had fought as allies only weeks before, did at least have the important effect of displaying British determination to the world, and not least to the neutral United States and its President, Franklin D. Roosevelt.

In the aftermath of the fall of France Churchill told his countrymen that: "Hitler knows that he will have to break us in this island or lose the war." Although Hitler was at first indifferent to the idea of invading England he soon warmed to the idea, and on July 16 he issued a directive outlining Operation *Sealion.* His navy began to assemble barges for the crossing, while the Luftwaffe prepared to fight for the air superiority upon which it would hinge. Some German historians have emphasized that *Sealion*'s chances were so poor than it cannot be taken seriously, and one has written: "The navy unquestionably gave *Sealion* no chance of succeeding."

The essential preconditions for invasion were never achieved. In mid-August the Germans, their bases now far closer than had ever been envisaged by prewar British planners. If they had weight of numbers on their side, they were handicapped by the fact that radar, some of it installed in the very nick of time, gave warning of their approach, and that the balance of pilot attrition told against them because much of the fighting took place over British soil. While RAF pilots who crash-landed or escaped by parachute were soon back in the battle (sometimes the same day) Germans who baled out over Britain were captured. Nor was German strategy well-directed, and for this Hermann Göring, Commander-in-Chief of the Luftwaffe, must shoulder much of the blame. Early in September, at the very moment that the RAF's battered airfields were creaking under the strain, the weight of the air campaign was shifted to Britain's cities. Black Saturday, September 7, was the first day of the air offensive against London, and although the blitz left an enduring mark on the capital and its population, it did not break morale. It was a terrible portent for the future. In December Air Marshal Arthur Harris, later to be commander in chief of the RAF's Bomber Command, stood on the Air Ministry roof with Sir Charles Portal, later chief of the air staff, and watched the city of London in flames. As they turned to go, Harris said: "Well, they are sowing the wind ..."

NORWAY

Neutral Norway attracted both Allies and Germans. The northern port of Narvik was the only all-weather outlet for Swedish iron ore, important to Germany, and deep-water channels along the coast, known as the Leads, formed a valuable link between Germany and the North Atlantic. The Allies contemplated seizing Narvik, pushing on to the ore-fields and then aiding the Finns, but resolved to mine the Leads instead. No sooner had they begun, on April 8, than it became clear that a major German invasion was under way: neither fierce Norwegian resistance nor a series of botched Allied counter-moves could prevent German occupation, completed by early June.

ABOVE
On February 16, 1940, *Graf Spee*'s homeward-bound supply ship *Altmark* was boarded by men from HMS *Cossack* in Jössing Fjord, in Norwegian territorial waters. Almost 300 prisoners were freed, but the incident strained Anglo–Norwegian relations and drew Hitler's attention to the area.

ABOVE

German soldiers disembarking in
Norway on April 9, 1940. They used
a variety of warships and civilian vessels
and achieved almost total surprise.

RIGHT

German troops landed by sea at Narvik
on April 9, but the Royal Navy attacked
and in two engagements, on the April 9
and 13, all German warships and
supply vessels were sunk or beached.

OPPOSITE PAGE
Norwegian soldiers at Kongsvinter, north-east of Oslo, where they resisted a German attack on April 28.

RIGHT
French troops embarking for Norway.

BOTTOM
German air power played a crucial role. This photograph shows a Bofors light anti-aircraft gun defending a Norwegian port: large quantities of ammunition and extemporized defences (fish-boxes filled with rubble) testify to its authenticity.

OVERLEAF
Many of the German troops involved in the campaign were from elite mountain divisions. These are using rubber assault boats to cross a fjord.

LEFT

Gloster Gladiators of 263 Squadron RAF lie burnt out on the frozen Lake Lesjaskog after a German air attack.

BELOW

British prisoners are marched off under guard. Many British troops involved in the campaign were not only poorly equipped and inadequately trained, but were committed to unrealistic plans.

CHURCHILL BECOMES PRIME MINISTER

Churchill had joined the War Cabinet as First Lord of the Admiralty on the outbreak of war, and replaced Chamberlain as Prime Minister in the furore that followed the disastrous Norwegian campaign. Here he confers with Gort and his Chief of Staff, Lieutenant General Pownall. The latter pointed out in his diaries that it was not easy to work with Churchill. "Can nobody prevent him," he wrote on May 24, "trying to conduct operations himself as a sort of super Commander-in-Chief?" However, Churchill's energy and resolve had a terrific impact on the British war effort: his flaws, like his strengths, were on a grand scale, but he was the man of the hour. This image was taken in France on November 5, 1939, while Churchill was still First Lord of the Admiralty.

Holland refused to give way to a German ultimatum, and was duly invaded. Surrender negotiations were under way on May 14, but news failed to reach the German aircraft that bombed Rotterdam, destroying part of the city centre and killing over 800 civilians.

GERMANY INVADES THE LOW COUNTRIES AND FRANCE

The Germans considered a number of plans for the invasion of France and the Low Countries. Hitler eventually backed the most ambitious, which concentrated the main weight of armour in a major thrust through the Ardennes. This struck the hinge between the static French forces in the Maginot Line and the north-eastern wing of Allied armies, part of which was to move forward into Belgium as soon as the Germans attacked. The offensive began on May 10, 1940, and the Germans crossed the Meuse at Sedan on the May 14, driving on to reach the Channel coast near Abbeville on May 20.

The Dutch surrendered on May 14. Here a Dutch officer, still wearing a sword, in an echo of more chivalrous times, is interrogated by his captors.

Belgium remained scrupulously neutral, denying access to British and French troops, until the invasion began. Here British infantry cross the frontier near Roubaix on May 10.

ABOVE

The powerful Belgian fortress of Eben
Emael covered the Albert canal just south
of Maastricht. German airborne troops,
shown here in the elation of victory, landed on
top of it in gliders, destroyed many guns and
observation slits, and forced the numerically
superior garrison to surrender on May 11.

RIGHT

The first attackers crossed the Meuse
on May 14 in rubber boats under cover of
a heavy land and air bombardment.
Only when the far bank was secure
could bridges be built to take tanks across.

ABOVE
An unposed action shot, with the photographer sensibly placed, showing a German anti-tank gun engaging French troops in the trees lining the road near Handainville, June 15, 1940.

BELOW
The field telephone remained at the heart of communications in 1940. A German NCO mans a telephone exchange in a roadside slit trench.

OPPOSITE, TOP
A British field gun in action May 30–31.
German air superiority made artillery
deployed in the open especially vulnerable:
this gun enjoys the benefit of some cover.

OPPOSITE, BOTTOM
A member of the German 56th
Artillery Regiment, on his way to
the Channel coast, took this photograph
of refugees killed in an air attack.

ABOVE
French prisoners in a
makeshift camp, summer 1940.

LEFT
Exhausted Belgian troops on
the Louvain–Brussels road.
All European armies except
the British used substantial
numbers of horses in 1940.

ABOVE
In an image taken near Louvain, refugees
make their way to safety, May 1940.

DUNKIRK

The German breakthrough left the BEF, the Belgian army and substantial French forces encircled. On May 25, Gort decided that his position was untenable and issued orders for a withdrawal through Dunkirk, a controversial decision which many Frenchmen regarded as betrayal. Bertram Ramsay, Vice-Admiral Dover, had begun plans for the evacuation of limited numbers of specialists, and was able to increase the scale of the rescue, aided by unusually fine weather. A total of 338,000 men, 120,000 of them French, were evacuated from Dunkirk itself and the open beaches to its east.

LEFT

The Admiralty increased its Small Vessels Pool by appeals broadcast by the BBC, and dozens of "little ships", many crewed by their owners, helped evacuate troops from Dunkirk. These, photographed on the Thames on June 4, survived the experience, though all too many did not.

BELOW

Many troops waited under intermittent air attack on the beaches between Dunkirk and La Panne: the skipper of the *Little Shamrock* said they looked "like thousands of sticks." They were ferried out to waiting ships in an assortment of small craft.

RIGHT
There were two long and relatively fragile moles protecting Dunkirk harbour, and on May 27, large vessels began to evacuate troops from the east mole. Here soldiers board HMS *Harvester* from the mole.

BELOW
French, Belgian and Dutch vessels also played their part. Here the French destroyer *Bourrasque*, loaded with troops, sinks off Dunkirk.

OPPOSITE
Destroyers were the workhorses of the evacuation, and six were sunk: HMS *Wakeful* went down in seconds with 650 troops aboard. These men are more fortunate, and have reached Dover, where the majority of evacuees disembarked.

The Isle of Man steam packet *Mona's Queen* took 1420 men home on May 26, but was sunk three days later.

Survivors from *Mona's Queen* coming alongside HMS *Vanquisher*.

The reality of evacuation: dishevelled but grateful survivors at Dover.

And the necessary myth: the tea, sandwiches and captured German helmet underline the propaganda value of this photograph.

ABOVE
Abandoned anti-aircraft guns – the
BEF lost all its heavy equipment –
and shrouded dead at Dunkirk.

OPPOSITE, TOP
Jetsam of defeat: a dead
Allied soldier on the beach.

OPPOSITE, BOTTOM
German troops securing Dunkirk.

ABOVE
German air power was dominant throughout the campaign. The Junkers Ju 87 Stuka dive-bomber with its characteristic gull-winged silhouette, acted as "flying artillery" for advancing German tanks.

THE FALL OF FRANCE

The French garrison of Lille fought on while the Dunkirk evacuation proceeded, but with the collapse in the north the Germans regrouped and struck southwards. There was more heavy fighting in the often-neglected part of the campaign. The 51st Highland Division, a fine Scots Territorial formation which had been fighting under French command, was forced to surrender at St Valéry-en-Caux on June 12. The Germans entered Paris on June 14, and on June 22, an armistice was signed at Rethondes, in the Forest of Compiègne – scene of the 1918 armistice negotiations.

RIGHT

A Fiesler Storch flies over tanks of the 7th Panzer Division, halted briefly in a valley just south of the Somme, June 1940.

BELOW

Major General Erwin Rommel, Commander of 7th Panzer Division, in satisfied mood at St-Valéry, 12 June. A grim-faced Major General Fortune of the 51st Highland Division stands behind him.

ABOVE
French colonial units fought, some with
great distinction, in the 1940 campaign:
these African troops have become prisoners.

RIGHT
CBS correspondent William Shirer (centre)
types his account of the armistice.
In the background is the hall which
had housed the railway carriage in
which the 1918 ceremony was concluded.
The carriage was taken to Germany
where it was destroyed in an air raid.

OPPOSITE
Discarded French helmets and gas
masks, both dating from an earlier war.

ABOVE
In one of the campaign's most
durable images (note the film
truck in the background) German
troops parade through Paris.

ABOVE
A German officer discussing
arrangements with a Spanish policeman
on the Franco–Spanish border.

OVERLEAF
Hitler triumphant on his only
visit to Paris, June 23, 1940.

THE OCCUPATION OF
THE CHANNEL ISLANDS

The Channel Islands were the only part of the United Kingdom to be occupied by German forces. The two main islands, Jersey and Guernsey were bombed on June 28, and German troops began unopposed landings two days later. The occupation was in fact harsher than was once suggested, and there is evidence of collaboration by the islands' authorities in round-up and deportation of Jews. This uncomfortable image, with its heavy propaganda message, shows a policeman opening the door for the German commandant of the Channel Islands, whose hotel headquarters on Guernsey still bears the Automobile Association emblem awarded in happier times.

FRANCE

On the night of 16–17 June the French government formed
by Marshal Philippe Petain requested an armistice. But not
all Frenchmen were prepared to accept it. Charles de Gaulle,
a recently-promoted brigadier general who had fought with
some success in the campaign, left for England, and on June 18,
he broadcast on the BBC, urging his countrymen to continue
the fight on, and ten days later the British recognized him as the
leader of all free Frenchmen. The relationship between Churchill
and de Gaulle was never comfortable, but thanks to de Gaulle
the flame of France's national honour was kept alight.

ABOVE
Charles de Gaulle accompanies King
George VI in an inspection of Free
French troops, summer 1940.

BELOW
Marshal Petain, head of the French
state established at the spa town of
Vichy, shaking hands with Hitler.

LEFT

The British were concerned that the French fleet, the fourth largest in the world, would fall into German hands. This photograph shows part of a powerful squadron, including the modern battle-cruisers *Dunkerque* and *Strasbourg*, in the Algerian port of Mers-el-Kebir.

BELOW

The British demanded that the ships at Mers-el-Kebir should join the British fleet or be scuttled, handed over or neutralized; they attacked when the French, hardly surprisingly, refused. The old battleship *Bretagne* blew up and *Dunkerque* was crippled: almost 1300 French sailors died. This very painful incident caused the Vichy government to break off relations with Britain, but it showed the international community just how determined the British now were.

The battle of France was still being fought when these little evacuees left London: a policeman is checking one little tot's label to make sure she boards the right train.

Signposts and other direction indicators which would have helped invaders to find their way around the country were taken down.

BRITAIN PREPARES

With the fall of France Britain stood alone, and Churchill presciently informed his countrymen that Hitler would have to "break us in this island or lose the war." Serious preparations were made to meet an invasion, although, with so much of its equipment lost in France, the army was pitifully weak.

The evacuation of children from London and other major cities, begun the previous year but reversed (despite government pleas) as many children returned to the cities when air attacks did not materialize, resumed, and Britain braced itself for a long war.

LEFT

Most evacuees soon found their feet. These children, photographed in the winter of 1940–41, are from the home at Kilronan, funded by money raised by the Junior American Red Cross.

RIGHT

Beach defences transformed the British coast. These little girls look wistfully at the wired-off sand.

LEFT

When Churchill was asked what should be done with "enemy aliens", German and Italian citizens in England at the outbreak of war (many of them refugees, Jewish and non-Jewish), his reply was characteristic: "Collar the lot." Here on May 29, women and children, escorted by police and officials, board a train which will take them to internment on the Isle of Man.

ABOVE
Saucepans into Spitfires. With Britain's isolation, some key raw materials became scarce, and householders were urged to give up aluminium cooking utensils for recycling.

RIGHT
There was much emphasis on "business as usual", and the original caption to this 1940 photograph points out that these bales of woollens are being exported.

OVERLEAF
On May 15, Churchill asked President Roosevelt for the loan of American destroyers. Roosevelt was initially negative, but once he had been nominated for a third term in office and seen British determination at Mers-el-Kebir, he authorized a "destroyers for bases" agreement. Although only nine destroyers were delivered by the end of 1940 their portent was enormous. These sailors are British, but two have obtained caps from their vessel's original US Navy crew.

THE AIR WAR

There was no pause in the war in the air. Even before the Battle of Britain proper began, British and German aircraft attacked shipping and the RAF mounted raids, often using leaflets rather than bombs, on Germany.

ABOVE
An RAF raid on an airfield in northern France. Two Focke-Wulf Fw58 Weihe aircraft are clearly visible.

RIGHT
An RAF crewman prepares to unleash leaflets onto Germany.

OPPOSITE
In late June 1940 a Blenheim bomber flies over a blazing German tanker in the Channel.

THE DEFENCE OF THE REALM

"Don't you know there's a war on?" was a common rejoinder in wartime Britain, but by the summer of 1940 it was impossible not to know it. Defence precautions went on apace, Local Defence Volunteers (later called the Home Guard) were formed, and there was a whiff of invasion in the air.

ABOVE
Royal Marine guards, at the entrance to the Admiralty, looking across Horse Guards Parade.

LEFT
Farm machinery and fencing form barricades in a Northumberland village, June 6.

BELOW
European governments-in-exile in Britain had their own armed forces: here Czech leader Dr Eduard Benes reviews his troops at Cholomondley Park, near Chester in July.

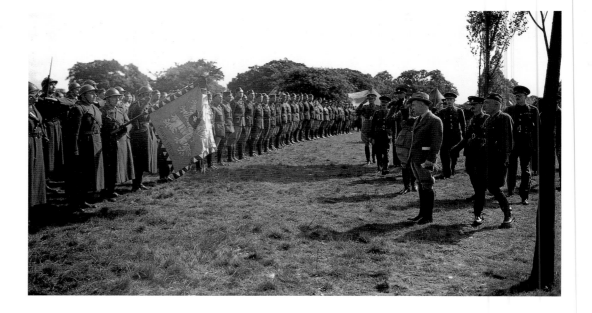

ABOVE
The formation of Local Defence Volunteers was announced on May 14, and within 24 hours a quarter of a million men had volunteered. This contingent has no equipment but distinguishing armbands, though several First World War veterans proudly wear their medals. The force was soon renamed the Home Guard, and its units were affiliated to the army's county regiments.

THE BATTLE OF BRITAIN

Invasion could not succeed without air superiority, and on July 10, the Luftwaffe began to attack shipping in the Channel. A week later Hitler issued orders for Operation *Sealion*, and in August bombers struck airfields of the RAF's Fighter Command. Both sides consistently over-estimated the number of enemy aircraft destroyed, but the RAF was never as badly weakened as the Germans supposed, and while German pilots who parachuted were captured, their British counterparts could fight on. In early September German efforts were fatally handicapped by Göring's diversion of resources to bombing cities, and *Sealion* was postponed on September 17.

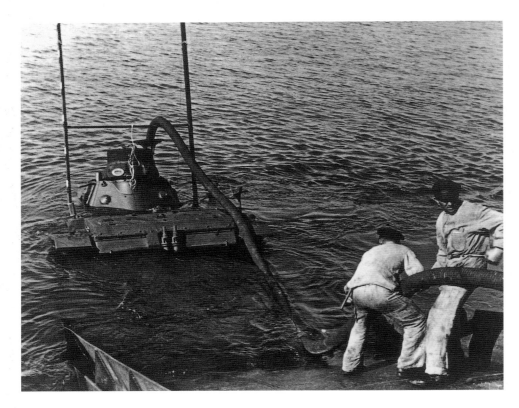

Preparations for Operation *Sealion*, the intended German invasion of Britain, included experiments with amphibious tanks.

A Women's Auxiliary Air Force (WAAF) operator plots targets. Primitive radar was heavily dependent on skilled users.

There were 20 "Chain Home" radar stations, whose 300-ft masts enabled the detection of high-altitude long-range targets. The twelve sites of "Chain Home Low", for lower targets, became operational only in July 1940.

ABOVE

The Operations Room at RAF Bentley Priory, Fighter Command's headquarters. Symbols representing squadrons are moved across the map, while senior officers in the gallery above control the battle.

LEFT

Civilian volunteers of the Royal Observer Corps reported the numbers, direction and type on incoming aircraft. Here an observer plots the height of a German formation.

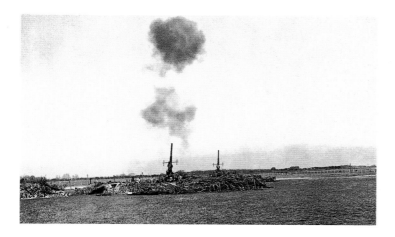

ABOVE
Tethered barrage balloons were flown on likely approaches to targets, forcing attackers to remain above them to avoid hitting their cables.

LEFT
The 3.7-inch gun was the mainstay of anti-aircraft defence. Batteries generally fired a barrage of shells, fused to bust at the estimated height of approaching aircraft, into the attackers' path.

FOLLOWING PAGES
Pilots of the Spitfire-equipped 610 Squadron await the order to scramble at RAF Hawkinge on the south coast in July.

ABOVE
Pilots relied on hard-working ground
crew. Here the wing-mounted
machine-guns of a Hurricane Mk 1
are re-armed: care is taken to avoid jam-
inducing kinks in the belted ammunition.

RIGHT
Two Hurricanes from 501 Squadron
scramble from Hawkinge, August 16.
Although the Hurricane was slower than
the more modern Spitfire, it nevertheless
played a distinguished part on the battle.

OPPOSITE
One of the war's classic photographs:
A Heinkel He 111 over Wapping on
"Black Saturday", September 7, the
first day of the offensive against London:
300 tons of bombs were dropped and about
2,000 civilians killed or seriously injured.

Lieutenant Karl-Heinz Thurz at
the controls of a Heinkel He 111 bomber.

RIGHT
The camera guns of an RAF fighter
record the end of a Junkers Ju 87 Stuka.

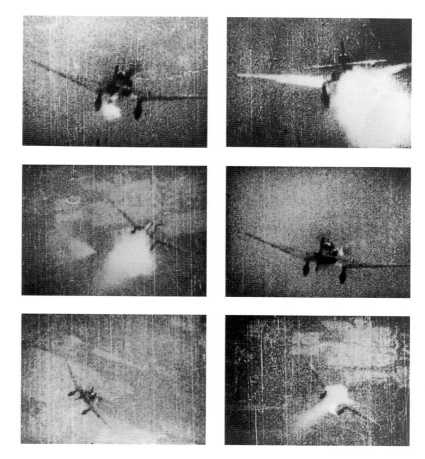

BELOW
Spectators at the wreckage of a Dornier
Do 17, shot down on August 12. Between
July 10 and October 31 the Luftwaffe lost
some 1,294 aircraft to the RAF's about 788.

LEFT
The Blitz did not just hit London
and major provincial cities like
Bristol and Liverpool. Here Churchill
inspects bomb damage in little Ramsgate.

THE BLITZ

The Blitz – an abbreviation of blitzkrieg (lightning war) – was
the name given to German attacks on British cities in 1940–41.
London was bombed by accident on the night of August 24, and
the RAF responded by bombing Berlin the following night. In early
September, Göring unwisely shifted the Luftwaffe's main effort from
airfields to cities, and "Black Saturday", September 7, saw the first
major raid on London. When the Blitz ended in May 1941, over
43,000 civilians had been killed and great tracts of ancient cities and
industrial centres devastated: but popular resolve had not been broken.

OPPOSITE PAGE
On the night of December 29–30, the City of
London was devastated by incendiary bombs:
the Guildhall and eight Wren churches were
among the buildings destroyed. The survival of
St Paul's Cathedral was little short of miraculous,
and the photographs of it rising above the
ruins somehow typified London's spirit.

RIGHT
On November 13, German bombers struck
Coventry in the midlands, destroying not only
twelve armaments factories but also part of the
city centre and the 14th-Century cathedral.

ABOVE
The phrase "fires were started"
became a standard feature of wartime
news broadcasts. Here firemen
work on a blaze in the City of London.

ABOVE

The photographer Bill Brandt had studied with Man Ray in Paris before returning to England to make a series of social records contrasting the lives of rich and poor. He worked for the Ministry of Information during the Blitz: this photograph shows a Sikh family sheltering in London's East End.

OPPOSITE PAGE

London Underground stations were used as air raid shelters. The authorities disapproved of the practice at first, but then did what they could to make them more comfortable, and life underground soon developed its own culture. These Londoners are sleeping on the escalators in one London tube station.

RIGHT

Mimicry of death: shop dummies lie on the pavement after the London department store was hit in 1940.

BELOW

At the height of the Blitz most of the 1,500,000 people serving in the various fire, civil defence, shelter and casualty organizations were part-time volunteers. Here a rescue party – with the double R designation on its steel helmets – removes a Blitz victim from rubble.

THE ITALIANS IN NORTH AFRICA

The Italians had a quarter of a million men under Marshal Balbo in Libya. Balbo was shot down by his own anti-aircraft guns over Tobruk and his successor, General Graziani, advanced cautiously to the Egyptian frontier where he prepared a line of forts. On December 7, Major General O'Connor began a large-scale raid on the forts with his Western Desert Force of 31,000 men. On December 9, the forts were taken and the coast road was cut between Sid Barrani and Buq-Buq behind them. O'Connor converted the raid into a sustained advance, overrunning the whole of Cyrenaica and taking some 130,000 prisoners.

ABOVE
Light tanks of the commanding officer and adjutant of the 4th Hussars on their way to Buq-Buq, December 11.

BELOW
The desert was often rocky, and at night its temperature dropped. These British troops in a defensive position at Bardia on December 31, 1940 are wearing greatcoats.

LEFT
Mines were widely used in the desert. Here men of the of the 1st Battalion The South Staffordshire Regiment are laying anti-tank mines in a position running towards the Mediterranean, October 1940.

BELOW
December 10, 1940. An Italian strides off into captivity with his dog.

1941

THE WAR TAKES SHAPE

THE YEAR 1941 SHAPED THE SECOND WORLD WAR, AND, ALTHOUGH IT WOULD HAVE TAKEN REMARKABLE PRESCIENCE TO PREDICT ITS OUTCOME, ITS REAL PATTERN WAS EMERGING. WHEN THE YEAR OPENED BRITAIN STOOD ALONE AGAINST GERMANY, AND IF THE BATTLE OF BRITAIN HAD DEMONSTRATED THAT THE GERMANS COULD NOT MOUNT A SUCCESSFUL INVASION, THE TOLL INFLICTED ON MERCHANT SHIPPING BY GERMAN SUBMARINES WARNED OF A PERIL THAT WAS SCARCELY LESS GREAT.

THE UNITED STATES remained neutral, but this neutrality wore increasingly thin, with the Lend-Lease bill becoming law in March and Churchill and Roosevelt meeting to sign the Atlantic Charter off Newfoundland in August.

Britain's fortunes ebbed and flowed. In North Africa Major General Richard O'Connor's Western Desert Force began Operation *Compass* on December 9, 1940, first overrunning Italian positions on the Egypt–Libya border and then exploiting success in a campaign which took some 130,000 prisoners and pressed round the bulge of Cyrenaica as far as Beda Fomm. This was not an isolated Italian defeat, for in the spring of 1941 the Duke of Aosta's substantial army in Eritrea, Abyssinia and Somaliland was attacked by two British forces. Lieutenant General Sir William Platt jabbed down from the Sudan, and won a bitterly contested action at Keren. Lieutenant General Sir Alan Cunningham thrust up from Kenya, first forcing the Juba River, on the border of Italian Somaliland, and then swinging north to Harar, within striking distance of the Abyssinian capital Addis Ababa. The Italians abandoned the city on April 4th, and the Duke of Aosta, whose troops had fought with courage and chivalry, formally surrendered at Amba Alagi in May.

General Sir Archibald Wavell, the British Commander-in-Chief in the Middle East, faced problems elsewhere. Iraqi rebels besieged the RAF base at Habbaniya, and a column, sent from Palestine to relieve it, went on to take Baghdad, re-establishing political equilibrium. The Vichy French garrison of Syria and the Lebanon had provided equipment to the Iraqis, allowed German aircraft to land in Syria, and bombed Habbaniya. On June 8, a force under General Sir Henry Maitland Wilson invaded, with British and Australian troops moving through the Lebanon and an Indian division striking from Northern Iraq. Despite expectation that Vichy forces would not fight hard, for there were Free French units with the Allied force, the reverse was true. The courage of the defence was in part inspired by a desire to demonstrate that French soldiers should not be judged by the debacle of 1940, and it was not until mid-July that an armistice was signed. It allowed French soldiers to choose between repatriation and service with Free French forces, and the majority chose to go home. Lastly, the danger of German penetration of Iran inspired a joint Anglo–Russian invasion mounted, in August, with little loss of life.

Wavell was less successful elsewhere. Early in the year he was ordered to send over 50,000 men and several RAF squadrons to support Greece, threatened by Axis attack. The Greeks saw off the initial Italian invasion, but on April 6, the Germans, joined by Bulgaria, invaded Greece and Yugoslavia. Although many Yugoslavs fought on despite their government's surrender, Axis occupation of the Balkans, completed in May, was a setback for Britain. It did, however, contribute to German overextension, and it has been argued that it delayed Operation *Barbarossa*, the German invasion of Russia, extending what began as a victorious campaign into a punishing Russian winter.

The Germans pressed their advantage, and mounted a bold airborne operation to secure the island of Crete whence they hoped to launch air attacks on British shipping in the eastern Mediterranean. It began on May 20, and although Lieutenant General Sir Bernard Freyberg's garrison of British, Australians and New Zealanders fought hard, the battle turned, as battles often do, on a small issue, and German ability to reinforce through the single airfield of Málame proved decisive. The Royal Navy dealt with seaborne invasions, but at terrible cost, and the fighting demonstrated the vulnerability of ships to air attack. Such was the damage inflicted on German airborne forces, however, that they never again mounted a large-scale airborne assault.

The scale of O'Connor's victory had persuaded Hitler to send a small German detachment to Africa under Erwin Rommel, who had made his reputation in France in 1940. The nucleus of what became the Afrika Korps was intended to block further British advance, but Rommel lost no time in going onto the offensive, striking on March 31, and then dividing his force at Agedabia, sending part of it around the coast road and the rest across Cyrenaica, capturing O'Connor himself and much of the 2nd Armoured Division, one of whose brigades had been sent to Greece. The port of Tobruk held out, with its largely Australian garrison. The British struck back in May, first launching an abortive attack on Sollum, and then, in June, mounting Operation *Battleaxe* in an effort to get through to Tobruk. Although the British made some progress, they were no match for Rommel, and Churchill decided to replace Wavell with General Sir Claude Auchlinleck, appointing Cunningham, victor in Abyssinia, to command the newly-formed 8th Army.

The rival forces were more or less evenly matched when, on November 18, Cunningham launched Operation *Crusader*. It started well, with British armour taking the dominating ground at Sidi Rezegh. Rommel then launched a characteristically bold stroke, hooking through to the Egyptian frontier, causing a panic and persuading Cunningham to fall back. Auchinleck at once counter-manded the move and replaced the exhausted Cunningham by Lieutenant General Neil Ritchie. In late November the British renewed their efforts, this time pushing Rommel out of Cyrenaica and relieving Tobruk.

The pattern of the desert war had emerged. Both sides were largely dependent on the sea for supplies and reinforcements, whose arrival reflected the shifting importance attributed to the theatre by Hitler and Churchill. On the ground the British usually had the advantage of numbers in both men and tanks. Although the Germans did not enjoy the clear qualitative lead in tank technology once attributed to them their tanks were generally more robust and battleworthy and their all-arms tactics far more consistent. And in Rommel they had a commander who understood the medium of desert war like few of his opponents. Logistics were profoundly influential within the theatre itself, and the switchback character of advances and retreats was partly dictated by the fact that successful attackers outran their logistics. Finally, long lines of communication and an open landscape placed air power at a premium, and while the Luftwaffe was comfortable in its role of ground support arm, the Western Desert Air Force (weakened, like the army, by diversions to Greece) had not yet found its balance.

On June 22 the Germans began Operation *Barbarossa*, the invasion of Russia. This was a significant widening of the war, and the apogee of that strategic overextension which was ultimately to bring Germany down. Despite the *rapprochement* of 1939, Hitler had always envisaged dismembering the Soviet Union, excising Bolshevism and opening up *Lebensraum* (living space) in the east. The war's political content made it, from the very start, an ideological conflict to which normal standards of behaviour did not apply. It also prevented the Germans from taking advantage of the anti-Russian and anti-Communist elements that were so widespread in the Soviet Union.

The initial attack saw three German army groups – North, Centre and South – plunge deep into Russia, with armoured spearheads breaking through the Russian defence and meeting behind to create vast pockets whose eventual reduction brought tens of thousands of prisoners: in the Vyazma–Bryansk operation of September–October, for example, 663,000 men, 1,242 tanks and 5,412 guns fell into German hands. Although Stalin reacted ruthlessly, removing (and often executing) the incompetent or the unlucky, these setbacks were, in large measure, his fault. The Soviet army had been badly damaged by the purges of 1937; intelligence warnings of German intentions had been ignored; and Soviet deployment so close to the frontier (which has persuaded some historians that Stalin himself had aggressive intentions) had made the success of the great German envelopments more likely. Once battle was joined, Stalin's influence was often disastrous: he forbade the withdrawals which might have saved whole armies, appointed cronies to senior posts, and remorselessly overcentralized.

And yet, in part because of Stalin and in part despite him, Russia fought back, depriving the Germans of victory in the war's first campaign. The T-34, arguably the war's outstanding medium tank, and the Katyusha rocket-launcher both made an impressive debut. In August Stalin named himself as Commander-in-Chief, set up the Stavka of the Supreme Commander and charged it with directing military operations. Although, like much else Stalin did, this contributed to over-centralization, it also produced cohesive strategic direction. Hitler's errors made their own contribution to failure: he dithered over establishing clear strategic objectives, and, in the event, his forces secured neither Moscow nor Leningrad, whose capture would have had extraordinary psychological impact. Nonetheless, the Germans began their last offensive early in October and by the month's end they were at the gates of Leningrad in the north, only 30 miles (48 kilometres) from Moscow, in the centre, and in the south had taken the wheatfields of the Ukraine and all but overrun the Crimea. But, as the armoured expert General Heinz Guderian himself observed, "the bitterness of the fighting was telling on our officers and men", and there was "an urgent need for winter clothing of all sorts."

Although the Soviet government had left Moscow, Stalin stayed on, and his speeches of early November – the twenty-fourth anniversary of the revolution – recalled Churchill at his most stirring. The ruthless General G. K. Zhukov, who had masterminded the defeat of the Japanese at Khalkin-Gol in Manchuria in 1939, had been appointed Stalin's deputy Commander-in-Chief in 1941. Stalin sent him where the danger was greatest, first to Smolensk and then to Leningrad, and finally brought him back to mastermind the defence of Moscow, for which substantial reserves were husbanded. On December 6, the Red Army began a series of counter-offensives which, by January 1942, extended the whole length of the front.

Hitler personally took over from Field Marshal Walther von Brauchitsch, whose *Oberkommando das Heeres* (OKH – Army High Command) had exercised overall control of the Eastern Front, and ordered his troops to stand fast. His personal intervention proved decisive, and the episode did much to enhance Hitler's military reputation in his own (and some others') eyes. Yet it could not conceal the fact that Germany had not won a quick victory in the east.

Meanwhile, American relations with Japan continued to worsen, and after Vichy France agreed, in July, to the temporary occupation of French Indo-China by the Japanese, the USA froze Japanese assets, and both Britain and the Netherlands followed suit. Many Japanese now considered that there was no alternative between economic ruin and war, and in October 1941, Prince Konoye's cabinet, which had sought to compromise between the Americans and the military, resigned and was replaced by a hard-line government under General Hideki Tojo. When America declared that Japan must withdraw from China as a precondition for resumption of trade, Tojo declared that "one must be ready to jump with closed eyes from the veranda of the Kiyomizu Temple."

The Japanese leap consisted of a carefully co-ordinated attack on European possessions in the Greater East Asia Co-Prosperity Sphere, which began on December 7–8. Naval aircraft attacked the base of the US Pacific Fleet at Pearl Harbor on the Hawaiian island of Oahu, inflicting serious damage but neither rendering the base unfit for future use nor catching the American aircraft carriers, which were at sea at the time. Congress immediately voted for war, and the isolationists were silenced.

Elsewhere the Japanese swept all before them. They advanced through mainland China to take the British territory of Hong Kong, and pushed down through Malaya towards Singapore. American territories in the Pacific were snapped up, and although the Americans still retained a grip on the Philippines, the outlook was bleak across the whole of the Pacific. But even as 1941 ended, with the Allies surprised and outclassed, there were some Japanese who knew that it could not last. Admiral Isoroku Yamamoto, Commander-in-Chief of the Combined Fleet, had already warned: "we can run wild for six months or a year, but after that I have utterly no confidence."

WAR IN THE WESTERN DESERT

Italy had entered the war against France and Britain on June 10, 1940, following German successes in the west and she seemed likely to exploit her strong position in the Mediterranean. In September, Italian troops in Libya advanced to the Egyptian frontier, but in December a British attack not only overran Italian frontier positions but took the port of Tobruk and drove deep into Libya. In February 1941, however, German troops began to arrive, and soon, under their aggressive commander, Erwin Rommel, pushed the British back. For more than eighteen months the war in the Western Desert was to ebb and flow between El Agheila and El Alamein.

ABOVE
A pile of captured weapons marks the scale of the Italian defeat, January 1941.

RIGHT
A long column of disconsolate Italian prisoners winds its way into captivity.

Air power played a crucial role in the desert war. Here an Australian patrol of obsolescent Gloster Gladiators returns to its base near Bardia.

Port installations burning at Tobruk on January 24, 1941.

ABOVE

Lieutenant General Richard O'Connor (centre, middle distance), architect of the British victory, was captured by a German patrol in April 1941. Here he and Lieutenant Gen Philip Neame (centre) Major General Gambier Parry (in fur coat) and Brigadier Coombe (left) await transport to Italy.

BELOW

Both sides supplied their troops in North Africa by convoys which were vulnerable to sea and air attack. On March 28, 1941, an Italian squadron, hoping to intercept a convoy, instead encountered the British battle fleet off Cape Matapan. The Italians were slowed down by attack from the aircraft carrier HMS *Formidable*, and then badly mauled in a night battle. This unusual photograph, taken from a British Swordfish, shows an Albacore torpedo-bomber climbing just after releasing its torpedo at the heavy cruiser *Pola*.

RIGHT
A half-track of the Sd Kfz 251series
("Max") towing Rommel's caravan
("Moritz") near Tobruk, 1941.

BELOW
A British 5-inch gun, little changed since
the First World War, bombarding German
positions from besieged Tobruk, May 1941.

ABOVE

Cause. The 88 mm started life as an anti-aircraft gun, but was adapted to become the war's outstanding anti-tank weapon, with an effective range against tanks of up to 2000 metres and the ability to penetrate over 200 mm of armour at 500 metres. This gun is engaging British tanks at Mers el Brega on April 15, 1941, during Rommel's advance.

RIGHT

And effect? The heavy armour of the British Matilda Mk II tank made it invulnerable to many German anti-tank guns, but not to the 88 mm.

ABOVE
German tanks – mainly the
PzKpfw Mk II with a 20 mm
gun – on the move, June 1941
during the abortive Operation *Battleaxe*.

RIGHT
Rommel (left) in characteristic
pose, accompanied by his
Chief of Staff, Fritz Bayerlein.

Junkers Ju 87 Stuka dive bombers on their way to attack British tanks at Ghobi, November 23, 1941, during the hard fought but ultimately successful British offensive, codenamed Operation *Crusader*.

A classic image of the desert war. A British cruiser tank Mk VI Crusader, which compared well with its opponents although, with a 40 mm gun, relatively lightly-armed, passes a burning PzKpfw Mk IV during Operation *Crusader*, November 27, 1941.

THE BALKANS AND GREECE

The Italians invaded Greece in October 1940, and although the Greeks repelled the attack, the Germans concentrated in Romania for an assault of their own. Churchill, insistent that "the cradle of democracy" should be defended, ordered Wavell, Commander-in-Chief in the Middle East, to send troops from North Africa to Greece. More than 50,000 British, Australian, New Zealand and Polish troops were sent, gravely weakening Britain's grip on the Western Desert at just the time that Rommel was making his presence felt. On April 6, the Germans attacked Yugoslavia and Greece: the Yugoslavs surrendered on April 17 and the Greeks on April 24.

LEFT
British troops landing at Piraeus from HMS *Orion* and HMS *Ajax* in February 1941.

RIGHT

On March 1, Bulgaria joined the Tripartite
Pact of Germany, Italy and Japan.
The caption to this German photograph
of the march through Bulgaria recalls
"the armed brotherhood of the First World
War", when Bulgaria was a German ally.

BELOW

German tanks advancing through
Greece in April circumvent a
destroyed road by using railway tracks.

ABOVE

Elements of the SS motorized infantry division *Leibstandarte Adolf Hitler* under its tough commander Josef "Sepp" Dietrich pushing on through the tide of Greek prisoners, May 1941. *Leibstandarte* subsequently became a panzer division with a reputation for ruthlessness.

LEFT

The Germans invaded Yugoslavia on April 6, and the Yugoslav government surrendered eleven days later. These German citizens of Sarajevo present the "tablet of shame" commemorating the assassination of the Archduke Franz Ferdinand, the spark which ignited the First World War, to the invaders. It was sent on to Berlin.

CRETE

Hitler decreed that Crete would be taken to provide a base
for operations against British shipping. Operation *Mercury* was to
consist of a parachute and glider assault on Crete's three airfields –
Máleme in the west, Rethymnon in the centre and Iráklion to the
east – by General Kurt Student's XI Fliegerkorps with 7th Parachute
Division. Men of Fifth and Sixth Mountain Divisions would
then arrive by air and sea. When the landings began on
May 20, Lieutenant General Sir Bernard's Freyberg's British and
Commonwealth garrison of 31,000 men, including survivors from
Greece, fought back hard, but the defence was compromised by
failure to secure Máleme. German air supremacy also proved telling:
surviving defenders surrendered or were evacuated at the end of May.

ABOVE

Freyberg had won the Victoria Cross in the
First World War and enjoyed a reputation for
personal courage. During the battle for Crete,
however, he diverted some of his best troops
to meet a seaborne attack, probably as the
result of misreading a secret ULTRA message
(produced by British penetration of secret
German communications), thereby delaying
the crucial counterattack on Máleme airfield.

RIGHT

German Junkers Ju 52s dropping
parachutists under fire near Iráklion on May
20. 5th Airborne Division lost over 6,000
killed, wounded and missing: a shocked
Hitler forbade future airborne operations.

ABOVE
Troops from 5th Mountain Division at a
Greek airfield preparing to board Junkers
Ju 52s – the workhorse of German air
transport – to be flown in to Máleme,
relinquished by the defenders on May 22.

A Stuka attack on British shipping in
Suda Bay. Although the Royal Navy
destroyed or dispersed seaborne invasion
forces, it lost three cruisers and six
destroyers to air attack: seventeen
other ships were heavily damaged.

THE ATLANTIC CHARTER

In July 1941 presidential envoy Harry Hopkins told Churchill that President Roosevelt would like a personal meeting. Churchill grasped the opportunity to draw the USA closer to the beleaguered Britain. The meeting took place in early August off Newfoundland: Churchill arrived in HMS *Prince of Wales* and Roosevelt in USS *Augusta*. Roosevelt suggested a joint declaration of principles, and the Atlantic Charter, agreed on August 12, bound both states to forswear territorial aggrandisement, support self-determination and establish a peace bringing "freedom from want." Despite its bland tone, the Charter aligned the USA, though still technically neutral, firmly against Germany. One of the least-posed of a series of photographs of the meeting shows Roosevelt and Churchill with General George C. Marshall, US Army Chief of Staff (over Churchill's left shoulder) and, on Marshall's right, Admiral Ernest J.King, later Commander-in-Chief of the US fleet. The balding civilian in profile is US Under-Secretary of State Sumner Welles, who helped his British opposite number, Sir Alexander Cadogan, to prepare the Charter.

LEFT
An RAF armoured car from the Habbaniya base enters Fort Rutbah, Iraq, on May 16. There were few Germans and Italians in Iraq, and the pro-Axis elements in Iraq lacked both troops and a cohesive plan: Baghdad itself fell on May 31.

BELOW
After the German invasion of Russia, British and Russian troops jointly invaded Iran, where German influence was strong, in August 1941 to secure an overland route to Russia. A captured Iranian officer talks to a British officer, through an interpreter, near an Anglo–Iranian Oil Company refinery at the head of the Gulf.

THE MIDDLE EAST

A treaty permitted the stationing of British troops in Iraq, but in May the Iraqis, emboldened by Britain's misfortunes elsewhere, besieged the air base at Habbaniya. Churchill, concerned about the threat of oil supplies and the danger of German build-up, ordered Wavell to send troops from Palestine to relieve it, but when they arrived the siege had been lifted. In Syria and the Lebanon substantial French forces under General Dentz remained loyal to the Vichy regime. When they gave aid to the Iraqis and allowed German aircraft to land, the British decided to take action. Although Free French, as well as Australian, British and Indian units participated in the invasion, which began in June, Vichy troops fought with unexpected determination, and an armistice was not signed till July 14.

PREVIOUS PAGE

In Operation *Bishop*, mounted on the night of August 24, Indian army troops aboard HMS *Kanimbla* with an accompanying flotilla captured the Iranian port of Bandar Shahpur. The three groups of ships seen here are British and Indian warships alongside captured merchantmen.

ABOVE

An Anglo–Russian parade in Tehran, September 1941, the first contact between British and Russian soldiers during the war. General Novikov (Caucasus Army) and Brigadier Tiarks (9th Armoured Brigade) inspect Russian troops.

RIGHT

The British maintained a horsed cavalry brigade of one regular and two yeomanry regiments in Palestine. These yeomen ride along the coast road on their way into Syria on the last occasion that British cavalry went on campaign mounted.

LEFT

The unexpectedly sharp resistance put up by Vichy French troops created problems for British official war photographers, who largely confined themselves to shots of what the original caption terms "a picturesque scene." British troops are overshadowed by a giant irrigation waterwheel on the River Orontes at Hama.

BELOW

Armistice terms allowed French soldiers to choose between repatriation or service with the Free French. Much to de Gaulle's annoyance, only about 6,000 of Dentz's troops opted for Free France, while over 20,000 were repatriated. This photograph shows French soldiers waiting to register their preferences in Beirut.

HESS ATTEMPTS PEACE

Rudolf Hess drifted into politics after the First World War and quickly fell under the spell of Hitler, who he regarded as "the incarnation of pure reason." He became Hitler's deputy in 1933, but thereafter slipped out of the inner circle. On May 10, 1941, he flew to Scotland in an effort, he claimed, to negotiate peace between Britain and Germany, "two related northern states." Hitler, who almost certainly had no knowledge of the attempt, at once disclaimed him. At Nuremberg he received a life sentence for crimes against peace, and was incarcerated in Berlin's Spandau prison, where he committed suicide in 1987. This image shows RAF personnel posing with the wreckage of Hess's crashed Messerschmitt Bf 110.

LEND-LEASE

Though President Roosevelt was firmly convinced that Axis victory would be disastrous, isolationism in Congress and the electorate compelled him to proceed with caution. In December 1940 Churchill told him of the damage done by German submarines, and warned that the time was approaching when Britain would not be able to pay for munitions. The Lend-Lease bill, introduced into Congress in January 1941, empowered the president to transfer any defence material to any nation whose defence he believed vital to the USA's interests. Although isolationists fought hard, the bill became law in March, and proved a key turning-point in US foreign policy.

BELOW
British troops take refreshment in an American club, June 1941.

ABOVE
The propaganda value of Lend-Lease was enormous: here British schoolboys enjoy their eggs courtesy of Uncle Sam.

ABOVE

Although the Thompson sub-machine gun
was not an ideal military weapon, its American
symbolism, arising from prewar gangster films,
made it another propaganda coup. The British
soon replaced it by the cheaper and lighter
Sten, though it remained in limited service.

ABYSSINIA

In 1940 the Italians held Abyssinia and Eritrea with 350,000 men under the Duke of Aosta, and that summer they tightened their grip by overrunning British Somaliland. In December Wavell, Commander-in-Chief of the Middle East, met Lieutenant General Sir William Platt, commanding British forces in the Sudan, and Lieutenant General Sir Alan Cunningham, commander in Kenya, and sketched out plans for an advance into Eritrea from the north and Italian Somaliland and Abyssinia from the south. Platt's men took the fortress of Keren in March 1941, while Cunningham entered Addis Ababa in April. The Duke of Aosta surrendered at Amba Alagi on 18 May.

ABOVE
This photograph of a RAF Vickers Wellesley on its way to Keren suggests how the difficult terrain assisted the defenders. The Italians, including first-rate troops like Bersaglieri and Savoy Grenadiers, put up a stern resistance at Keren.

BELOW
The Emperor Haile Selassie re-entered his capital of Addis Ababa in May 1941. These men, heavily armed with captured Italian weapons, have gathered to hear the proclamation announcing his return.

LEFT
Surrender terms granted the Italians at Amba Alagi included the honours of war – the right to march out under arms, commanded by their own officers, before giving up their weapons. It was a fitting end to a campaign fought with what the military commentator J. F. C. Fuller called "marked chivalry."

BELOW
Enthusiastic members of a South African Transvaal Scottish regiment celebrating their entry into the Abyssinian capital.

THE SINKING OF THE BISMARCK

Grand Admiral Erich Raeder, Commander-in-Chief of the German navy, planned a two-pronged sortie into the North Atlantic by the battleship *Bismarck* and the heavy cruiser *Prinz Eugen* from the north and the battlecruisers *Scharnhorst* and *Gneisenau* from the French port of Brest. Damage to several vessels reduced this to a single thrust by the *Bismarck* group under Admiral Günther Lütyens. Although *Bismarck* and *Prinz Eugen* broke out into the Atlantic – sinking HMS *Hood* – *Bismarck* was caught making for France, damaged by air attack, battered into a hulk by superior British forces and either sunk by *Dorsetshire*'s torpedoes or scuttled by her crew.

ABOVE
Bismarck triumphant: the German battleship engaging the old battlecruiser HMS *Hood* in the Denmark Strait on May 24. A hit from one of the German warships caused a massive explosion which sank *Hood*: only three of her complement of 1,421 survived.

LEFT
Bismarck, on fire in the distance, engaged by the battleship HMS *Rodney* on May 27. Damage incurred in the Denmark Strait action had forced *Bismarck* to turn back, and an air-dropped torpedo had damaged her rudder. Although she shot well at the start of her final action, her inability to manoeuvre was a fatal disadvantage.

FOLLOWING PAGE
Survivors from *Bismarck* are pulled aboard HMS *Dorsetshire*. There were only 117 survivors from her company of 2,200: Admiral Lütyens was among those lost.

SPECIAL FORCES

In June 1940 Churchill suggested that 20,000 "Storm Troops" should be drawn from existing units, and the first commando raid was mounted near Le Touquet that month. Battalion-sized commando units were raised from volunteers, but it was not till March 1941 that the first major operation was mounted. Nos. 3 and 4 Commandos raided the German-held Lofoten Islands, destroyed fish oil factories, sank an armed trawler and a fish factory ship, took 220 prisoners and brought away 315 Norwegian volunteers, all without loss. Meanwhile, in the Western Desert, Lieutenant David Stirling, who had served in the commando "Layforce", pioneered what became the Special Air Service.

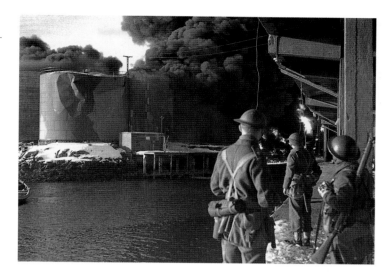

BELOW

Probably taken in January 1943, this photograph shows a jeep of the Special Air Service armed with twin .303 Vickers K guns (rear) and a forward-firing .5 machine-gun. Note the spare petrol carried in jerry cans – so called because they were copies of the German petrol can which replaced the aptly-nicknamed British "flimsy."

ABOVE

Oil storage tanks blazing during the commando raid on the Lofoten Islands, March 1941.

THE EASTERN FRONT

Despite his 1939 rapprochement with Stalin, Hitler never abandoned plans for an attack on Russia, which he planned to reduce to "a German India." In December 1940 he issued a directive for Operation *Barbarossa*, the invasion of the Soviet Union. His army was not ready for a long war: many units had French or Czech equipment and were below strength, and operations in the Balkans delayed the attack. Stalin had some warning of invasion, and the disposition of Russian forces, concentrated on the frontier, induces some historians to suggest that he planned an offensive of his own. The attack, on June 22, proved brilliantly successful, but ran out of steam in December, when the Russians launched serious counteroffensives.

OPPOSITE PAGE TOP
The cameraman's location and lack of uniformity amongst the gun detachment suggests that this shot of a German anti-tank gun taking on Soviet armour in July is authentic.

OPPOSITE PAGE BOTTOM
The German army remained two-tier, with its panzer and panzergrenadier divisions representing the tip of a spear whose shaft comprised units which would not have looked out of place a generation earlier. German cavalry crosses a bridge in Russia, summer 1941.

BELOW
German tanks form up for the attack on the open terrain that characterized much of the Eastern Front, July 1941.

Russia's broad rivers proved less of an
obstacle than their defenders expected.
Here German troops in rubber assault
boats cross the Dnieper in July, with
smoke on the far bank testifying to the
effect of air and artillery bombardment.

ABOVE

In Russia in 1941 the Germans profited,
as they had in Poland in 1939 and France
and the Low Countries in 1940, from
very effective air support. This shot shows
a camouflaged Russian airfield under what
the original caption terms "a hail of bombs."

RIGHT

The reality of the advance through Russia, September 1941. Most German soldiers, like their fathers and grandfathers, went into battle on foot, with horse-drawn transport.

BELOW

The German armoured thrusts into Russia linked to create vast pockets whose occupant defenders were captured: the Germans claimed over 400,000 prisoners by July 11.

ABOVE
A German machine gun post covers a street in Kharkov, taken by Rundstedt's Army Group South in October.

RIGHT
Narva, on the Gulf of Finland, had witnessed a Russian defeat by Charles XII of Sweden in 1700. Here German infantry pass beneath its old fortifications, September 1941.

FOLLOWING PAGES
Ukrainian peasants directing German soldiers. Much of the population of areas overrun by the Germans was not unsympathetic to the removal of the Soviet yoke: German failure to recognize this was a major political and strategic failure.

This photograph, released by the Russians in January 1942, shows the bodies of civilians shot by the Germans in a schoolyard at Rostov-on-Don.

German occupation was harsh and helped alienate national groups who had initially welcomed the Germans. This undated photograph, attributed by its original caption to a captured German soldier, shows a German officer hanging a prisoner.

ABOVE
The Russian counterattack of December used troops trained and equipped to operate in the sub-zero conditions. German commanders were badly shaken, and Hitler assumed personal command of the army, ordering his men to hold on regardless of cost.

RIGHT
A nation at war: members of the Moscow Young Communists digging an anti-tank ditch outside the Russian capital.

German prisoners captured
during the Russian winter offensive.

BELOW
Leningrad, now known by its old name
of St Petersburg, was encircled by the
advancing Germans, and in the
ensuing siege perhaps one million
soldiers and citizens died. These civilians
have been killed by German shelling.

ABOVE
The Russians kept Leningrad
supplied by running trucks
across the frozen Lake Ladoga.

PEARL HARBOR

In mid 1941 America reacted to Japanese occupation of French Indo-China by freezing Japanese assets. In October Prince Konoye's moderate cabinet was replaced by a government headed by General Tojo, and, despite the recognition by several leading figures that she could not win a long war, Japan prepared a devastating strike. On December 7, carrier-borne aircraft struck the US Pacific Fleet at Pearl Harbor, on the Hawaiian island of Oahu. Surprise was complete, although the Americans had received warnings which should have enabled them to meet the attack. American losses were heavy, but aircraft carriers were at sea and escaped the carnage.

Battleship row at Pearl Harbor.
From left to right are the USS *West Virginia*, *Tennessee* and *Arizona*. All three, along with the battleships *California* and *Nevada* eventually sank, but only *Arizona* and *Oklahoma* were total losses.

LEFT
The wreckage-strewn naval air station at Pearl Harbor during the Japanese attack.

BELOW
Anti-aircraft fire bursts among Japanese aircraft attacking the US Pacific Fleet. The Japanese lost 29 aircraft.

ABOVE

Small craft rescue survivors from the
battleship USS *California*, sunk
by Japanese aircraft. The Americans
suffered over 3,000 casualties in the attack.

RIGHT

Roosevelt denounced December 7 as
"a date which will live in infamy", and,
here, grim-faced, signs a declaration of
war against Japan. Some historians have
suggested that the Japanese attack gave
him a pretext for action he wished to take in
any event, but the extant evidence does not
prove his complicity in what may best be
seen as "the ultimate intelligence blunder."

JAPANESE ADVANCES IN SOUTHEAST ASIA

The raid on Pearl Harbor was part of a co-ordinated plan for attack on US, British and Dutch bases across a wide area. Japan's opponents were over-extended and ill-prepared, and the Japanese initially met with stunning success, snatching Malaya, Singapore and Hong Kong from the British, taking the American commonwealth of the Philippines and swamping the Dutch East Indies.

BELOW
Indian troops manning a coast defence gun at Hong Kong. Both Hong Kong and Singapore were well-provided with guns to face a naval threat, but lacked the resources to deal with an invasion from inland.

FOLLOWING PAGES
Canadian troops marching off after landing in Hong Kong in November 1941 to form part of its garrison.

BELOW
A classic shot of Japan triumphant
shows infantry charging into Hong Kong.

ABOVE
Hong Kong surrendered on December 25,
after an impossible battle against
confident and determined attackers.

Argyll and Sutherland Highlanders, supported by an armoured car, training for the defence of Malaya. One officer in the battalion observed that the tradition of certain country being "impassable to infantry" died hard, and in December 1941 the Japanese proved adept at hooking through the jungle behind road-blocks like this.

General Douglas MacArthur, Vice Commander-in-Chief of US and Philippine troops in the Far East, congratulates Captain Jesus Villamor of the Philippine Air Force for his bravery in the defence of the Bataan peninsula. MacArthur was eventually ordered to leave in March 1942, but vowed: "I shall return."

A Japanese propaganda photograph shows Allied prisoners queuing in order to record verbal messages to be sent home. Second from the right is Major James Devereux, commander of the US Marines on Wake Island and one of the heroes of the initial repulse of the Japanese on December 11: Wake fell to a heavier assault on December 23.

The modern battleship HMS *Prince of Wales* and the old battlecruiser HMS *Repulse* were sent to assist in the defence of Singapore and Malaya, but both were sunk by air attack on December 10. Here *Prince of Wales* goes to sea for the last time on December 8.

ABOVE
The crew of the stricken *Repulse* abandon
ship. Her commanding officer, Captain
Tennant, was saved, with 41 of his 69
officers and 734 of 1,240 ratings.

1942

THE TURNING POINT

THE YEAR 1942 WAS THE WAR'S TURNING POINT. AT ITS BEGINNING THE ALLIED POSITION LOOKED GRIM. IN THE EAST, THE GERMANS SOON RECOVERED FROM THE RUSSIAN WINTER COUNTEROFFENSIVE AND RENEWED THEIR ATTACK. ALL ACROSS THE PACIFIC THE JAPANESE CONTINUED TO RUN WILD, SNAPPING UP BRITISH AND DUTCH POSSESSIONS AND PRESSING THE ADVANTAGE OVER THE AMERICANS GAINED AT PEARL HARBOR.

IT WAS SMALL WONDER that General Sir Alan Brooke, newly-appointed Chief of the Imperial General Staff, wrote in his diary on New Year's Day: "Started New Year wondering what it may have in store for us … Will it be possible to ward off the onrush of Germany on one side and Japan on the other while the giant America slowly girds his armour on?"

Yet by the year's end the picture had changed dramatically. An entire German army was inches from destruction at Stalingrad. The power of the Japanese navy had been blunted at the Coral Sea and Midway. And not only had the Germans been decisively beaten at El Alamein, but Allied landings in French North Africa left little doubt that Axis forces would shortly be expelled from the entire continent. American industrial production was steadily gaining momentum, and American troops and aircraft were landing in a beleaguered Britain, in its fourth wearing year of the war, to prepare for an eventual assault on the mainland of Europe. The strategic bombing of Germany increased in pace, with the first ever thousand bomber raid launched on May 30. Somehow Churchill's post-Alamein pronouncement caught the mood of the year. "This is not the end," he declared. "It is not even the beginning of the end. But it is, perhaps, the end of the beginning."

It was in the Far East and the Pacific that the Allies' plight at first seemed worst. The Japanese accompanied their surprise attack on Pearl Harbor with attacks on other targets right across the theatre. They landed in Thailand and northern Malaya and pushed southwards against poorly co-ordinated British, Indian and Australian resistance, forcing the Johore straits to land on Singapore, where the British commander, Lieutenant General Arthur Percival, concluded the largest surrender in British military history. In the Philippines they destroyed over half General Douglas MacArthur's air force on the ground at Clark Field, near Manila, and then proceeded to invade. The courageous American and Filipino defence of the Bataan peninsula and the island of Corregidor bought time and honour but could not prevent the fall of the Philippines.

In January the Japanese invaded Burma, bundling the outmatched defenders back to take Rangoon on March 7 and cutting the land link between India and China. The longest ever British retreat saw the surviving defenders fall back to the very borders of India. An Allied naval squadron was trounced in the battle of the Java Sea on February 24, and the Dutch East Indies surrendered on March 8. In May, the Japanese attempted to invade New Guinea and take Port Moresby, but the Americans had breached their radio security and were ready for them: both sides lost a carrier apiece in the Battle of the Coral Sea. Worse was to come for the Japanese, for in early June they mounted an ambitious operation to lure part of the US Pacific Fleet northwards and bring the rest of it to battle around the island of Midway. Once again signals intercepted helped the Americans parry the blow, and in the ensuing battle the Japanese lost four carriers to the Americans' one.

Although the USA pursued the policy of "German first", emphasizing that the defeat of Germany would be her first strategic priority, she had sufficient resources to commit powerful forces to the Pacific. The theatre was divided into MacArthur's South-West Pacific Area, which included Australia, New Guinea, the Solomons, the Philippines and much of the Dutch East Indies. The tough and competent Admiral Chester W. Nimitz, commander of the US Pacific Fleet, was responsible for the Pacific Ocean Area. After Midway the Americans began a limited offensive, with the seizure of Guadalcanal and Tulagi in the southern Solomons leading to a vicious six-month battle for the former. Australian and US troops planned to advance up the north-east coast of New Guinea, but the Japanese landed at Buna and there was fierce fighting as they strove, unsuccessfully, to reach Port Moresby. Japanese forces on New Guinea had been weakened to send reinforcements to Guadalcanal, and although very fierce fighting was still in progress at the year's end, the issue could not be in doubt. And there was a sinister portent for the future. On April 18, Colonel James Doolittle led a force of B-25 bombers from the carrier USS *Hornet* in a raid on Japan. Although its material consequences were slight, in gave a much-needed boost to American morale.

On the Eastern Front the year began with *Pravda* confidently predicting German defeat that year. On the face of things there was reason for Russian optimism, for a general counteroffensive seemed to be making good progress against Germans who found the winter conditions decidedly unpleasant. However, the Russians were not yet sufficiently skilled to pull off operations on such a scale, and the Germans, buttressed by Hitler's demand for "fanatical resistance" held on. In the spring the Germans struck some deft blows of their own, netting tens of thousands more prisoners. In April, Hitler issued orders for Operation *Blue*, intending to demolish the remaining Soviet reserves and capture the oilfields of the Caucasus. The Germans made impressive progress, taking Rostov and nearing Stalingrad. Then Hitler declared that *Blue*'s mission was "substantially completed", and ordered two new operations, *Edelweiss*, a thrust into the Caucasus, and *Heron*, to secure the line of the Volga from Stalingrad to Astrakhan. Despite early promise the operations lost momentum, and at Stalingrad 6th Army became enmeshed in savage fighting in the ruins of the city.

Stalin, well aware that discipline and morale were fragile, applied both stick and carrot. Failure was punished remorselessly. The prestige of officers was enhanced and the authority of political commissars was curbed, decorations named after the heroes of old Russia and old-style epaulettes were soon to appear, and the Guards designation was revived and applied to units which had fought especially well. In late August he ordered Zhukov to plan the double envelopment of the German 6th Army. Operation *Uranus* began on November 19, and Russian spearheads broke through Romanian armies on both flanks of Stalingrad to meet east of Kalach on the Don. Although Hitler ordered Manstein, one of his ablest armoured commanders, to break through to the Stalingrad pocket the task was beyond even him, and Paulus, 6th Army's commander, surrendered on January 31 in the greatest German reverse to date.

A similar process of ebb and flow was evident in the Western Desert. In December 1941, Rommel had fallen back into Cyrenaica after losing the hard-fought *Crusader* battles. But he was not the man to remain there for long: as soon as he received more tanks and fuel he jabbed back, taking Benghazi and overrunning airfields from which attacks were stepped up on British convoys and the vital island of Malta. The 8th Army established itself in a well-prepared defensive line running from Gazala on the coast to the desert outpost of Bir Hacheim. Although ULTRA intelligence gave warning of an Axis attack, when Rommel launched Operation *Venezia*, hooking round the desert flank of the Gazala line, he mauled British armour which met him piecemeal and then had the better of bitter fighting in the Cauldron in the centre of the British position. From the British point of view Gazala was a battle of wasted opportunities. Many of the defensive "boxes" were very bravely held, and a Free French brigade distinguished itself at Bir Hacheim. But Lieutenant General Neil Ritchie, 8th Army's commander, lacked Rommel's deft touch: Tobruk fell on June 21, and by the end of the British were back behind the Egyptian frontier near the little railway halt of El Alamein.

Auchinleck, Commander-in-Chief in the Middle East, had already relieved Ritchie and taken personal command, and now he himself was replaced by General Sir Harold Alexander. Lieutenant

General William "Strafer" Gott was to have taken command of 8th Army but was killed in an accident, and Bernard Montgomery received the appointment instead. Historians argue whether Montgomery's repulse of Rommel's last attack at Alam Halfa between August 30 and September 7 owed much to preparatory work done in Auchinleck's time. In one sense the question is academic, for Rommel was now a sick man and his forces, yet again at the end of their logistic reach, were tired and over-extended.

Montgomery took pains to bring the Desert Air Force under his wing, stamped his confident mark on 8th Army, and made meticulous plans for his own offensive, launched on October 23. Rommel was on sick leave in Germany, and his stand-in died of a heart attack in the battle's early stages. Montgomery planned Operation *Lightfoot* to breach the German–Italian defences with infantry, and then pass his armour through to hold a line on which to blunt counterattacks, while the crumbling of the position went on. Progress was slow, but when Montgomery unleashed Operation *Supercharge*, his decisive blow, Rommel recognized that he was too weak to hold it and began to pull back his mobile units. Many static units, Italian for the most part, could not be extracted, and 30,000 prisoners were taken. The pursuit was hampered by poor weather and Montgomery's caution, but the battle broke the pattern of the war in the Western Desert: this time there would be no return to the see-saw of the past.

Montgomery's victory was encouraging for the Allies, who planned to invade French North Africa and then move eastwards so as to crush German and Italian forces in the theatre between these new armies and Montgomery. There was secret consultation to prevent French resistance, and American troops spearheaded the landings because it was thought that the French would be less likely to resist them than they would the British. Lieutenant General Dwight D. Eisenhower commanded the operation, in which three task forces struck in Morocco and Algeria on November 8. Unfortunately some French troops did fight back, and the navy resisted strongly. However, Marshal Petain's deputy Admiral Darlan, fortuitously in Algiers, concluded an armistice on November 10.

Petain at once repudiated the armistice, but an infuriated Hitler ordered German troops into the Unoccupied Zone of France. Darlan himself, now freed of his obligations to Vichy, was appointed high commissioner for French North Africa by Eisenhower, but was assassinated in December and replaced by the pro-Allied General Giraud. Darlan had attempted to persuade the powerful French fleet, based at Toulon, to join the Allies, but it declined to do so. However, when the German approached on November 27, Admiral Jean de Laborde ordered the fleet to be scuttled, and one battleship, two battlecruisers, seven cruisers and scores of smaller vessels were sunk. It was a tragic but courageous act, depriving the Germans of a prize which would have thrown a shadow over Allied operations in the Mediterranean.

The Germans now strained every nerve to hold North Africa, "the glacis of Europe." Reinforcements were rushed into Tunisia, forming what became Colonel General Hans-Jürgen von Arnim's 5th Panzer Army. Arnim blocked the way to Tunis, fighting the Allies to a halt in the atrocious weather of December. Victory in North Africa was not, as it had seemed at first to be, just round the corner, but at the year's end it seemed that even Arnim and Rommel, between them, could simply delay an inevitable defeat.

The Battle of the Atlantic changed character with American entry into the war. At first German submarines enjoyed a "happy time", as Allied shipping sailed, virtually unprotected, around the eastern seaboard of the USA: in May and June, they sunk over a million tons of shipping in American waters. The year saw the heaviest loss of Allied merchant shipping, over 6 million tons falling to U-boats. ULTRA, secret intelligence produced by British penetration of German ciphered radio communications, was crucial in the war against submarines, but for much of the year, a new cipher made U-boat signals safe. However, the extension of the convoy system, improvements in tactics and the extension of air patrols pointed the way to future success, and in December, British experts again cracked German messages. But there remained an "air gap" in mid-Atlantic, and the Germans, concentrating submarines in "wolf-packs", brought the battle to a crisis that would break in early 1943.

JAPANESE INVASION OF SINGAPORE AND MALAYA

After landing in Thailand and Malaya on December 8, 1941, the Japanese moved swiftly southwards and on January the causeway linking Singapore island with the mainland was blown by British engineers. On the night of February 8 the Japanese crossed the Johore Strait, and made good progress against a disorganized defence. Although Churchill had ordered that the battle should be fought "to the bitter end", the loss of much of the city's water supply persuaded Lieutenant General Arthur Percival to surrender. Churchill called the surrender, of some 85,000 men, "the worst disaster ... in British military history."

ABOVE

Singapore's coast defence guns, like this one, became the topic of ill-informed postwar criticism. They were designed to engage warships and so naturally pointed out to sea, though some could also fire inland. From 1937 British planners recognized that the main threat to Singapore came from landings to its north.

BELOW

Some women, children and key specialists were evacuated. The decision as to whether wives and children should be evacuated one was an agonizing one, and for many families this grim parting in Singapore's bomb-ravaged docks was the last.

Surrender negotiations began at 11.30 on
the morning of Sunday 15 February, when
a ceasefire was arranged. There was a surrender
ceremony in the Ford factory at Bukit Timah
that afternoon: the British delegation was
kept waiting outside before it began.

ABOVE
The propaganda impact of the surrender
was enormous, and the Japanese lost no
opportunity to drive it home. Here captured
soldiers are made to sweep the streets in
front of the native population.

BURMA

The fall of Malaya and Singapore left the Japanese free to turn their attention to Burma, where the British were to wage their longest Second World War campaign. Yet it was certainly not an exclusively British campaign, for Indian and African troops, along with combatants from many of Burma's indigenous peoples, fought in it, and American aircraft and special forces played their own distinguished part. Invasion proper began on January 19, 1942, the Japanese cut the land route between India and China on April, and by May the surviving defenders, now commanded by Lieutenant General "Bill" Slim, had reached the borders of India after a gruelling retreat.

BELOW
This photograph, which just predates the Japanese invasion, shows Indian troops, upon whom the defence of Burma largely depended, marching past a pagoda.

LEFT
Many Burmese, especially members of groups like the Karens, who tended to be pro-British, trudged north to escape the advancing Japanese in a dreadful odyssey which left thousands dead from disease, hunger and exhaustion.

BELOW
The British destroyed much equipment in order to prevent it from falling into Japanese hands: here the task of demolition goes on.

ABOVE
Although photographs like this were useful
for propaganda purposes, this shot of
Japanese entry into the southern Burmese
town of Tavoy makes the point that many
Burmese regarded Japanese invasion as an
opportunity to escape British rule.

BATAAN

Although the Philippines had become an autonomous commonwealth in 1935, in 1941 the United States integrated its armed forces into the American military, and General Douglas MacArthur, military adviser to the Philippine government, was recalled to active duty and appointed Far East army commander. The northern Philippines were invaded in December 1941, and, profiting from air and sea superiority, the Japanese soon overran the islands, with the exception of the Bataan Peninsula on Luzon and the island fortress of Corregidor. After brave resistance Bataan fell on April 9, 1942, and Corregidor on May 6. MacArthur himself, on Roosevelt's order, was evacuated in a fast patrol boat.

ABOVE
At the beginning of the war American troops, like their Filipino comrades-in-arms, wore British-style steel helmets.
This American soldier has a Molotov cocktail (a petrol-filled bottle ignited by a rag) for use against Japanese tanks.

BELOW
About 78,000 survivors of the fighting on Bataan were herded on a 65-mile (105-km) "death march" on which many of them died from exhaustion or the brutal treatment of their guards.

BELOW
American victims of the death march. In the controversial Far East war crimes trials the Japanese Lieutenant General Homma Masaharu was held responsible for the death march, whose excesses he blamed on officers under his command: he was executed on April 3, 1946.

THE BATTLE FOR THE PACIFIC

Japanese strategy in the Pacific was initially successful, and a short-lived ABDA (American–British–Dutch–Australian) Command collapsed before the Japanese advance. But although the Japanese won the battle of the Java Sea in February and hammered the British Admiral Somerville's Far Eastern Fleet on a raid into the Indian Ocean in April, they lost a carrier in the Coral Sea in May. The following month they lost four large carriers at Midway, and with them the prospect of maintaining the initiative in the central Pacific.

ABOVE

The cruisers HMS *Dorsetshire* and *Cornwall* under air attack, April 5: both were sunk. So great was the superiority shown by Japanese aircraft on the Indian Ocean raid that Somerville sent his elderly battleships to safety in the East African port of Mombasa.

The Battle of the Coral Sea was the first major naval action in which opposing warships did not sight one another. American aircraft sank the light carrier *Shoho*, but the USS *Lexington* – "Lady Lex" – was hit by bombs and torpedoes and sank after a huge internal explosion. Here members of her crew can be seen jumping from the stricken vessel.

In May the Japanese attacked the island of Midway, then America's most westerly outpost, having first diverted part of the US Pacific Fleet to the north. On June 4, Japanese aircraft attacked Midway, doing widespread damage and killing these servicemen.

Thereafter the Japanese plan went badly
wrong, and in the fierce battle that followed
three Japanese carriers were sunk and
another so badly damaged that she had to be
scuttled. Here US Douglas Dauntless planes
fly high above a burning Japanese carrier.

ABOVE
The carrier USS *Yorktown* at Midway
under air attack which damaged her
badly, leaving her to be finished
off by a submarine on June 7.

THE EASTERN FRONT AND STALINGRAD

In Russia the Germans survived the crisis of the Russian winter counteroffensive, and in April 1942 Hitler issued orders for Operation *Blue*, a major offensive in the south aimed at the oilfields of the Caucasus. In June the attack began well, with scenes reminiscent of victories the previous year, and the Germans pushed deep into the Caucasus. But by mid-September the offensive had stalled, and German 6th Army was making heavy weather of its attack on Stalingrad, on the Volga. On November 19, the Russians launched carefully husbanded reserves to began the attack which led to the encirclement of the 6th Army in one of the war's most terrible battles.

The Russian winter not only caught the Germans without proper clothing but caused serious difficulties for vehicles not designed with this climate in mind. Here a tank drags an assault gun from a snowdrift.

RIGHT
Although the Germans occupied the Crimea in 1941, the naval base of Sevastopol held out. It was eventually taken in July 1942 after heavy bombardments which reduced the city to rubble.

Sevastopol, besieged by the British and French in the Crimean War of 1854–56, was well-provided with modern defences. These women, described in the original caption as sewing underwear and warm clothing for the city's defenders, are probably sheltering beneath the older fortifications.

In early August 6th Army destroyed most of a Russian army in the bend of the Don north of Kalach. This is the apocalyptic scene on the river bank in the first week of August.

Operation *Edelweiss*, initiated when Hitler
cancelled Operation *Blue* in July, sent Army
Group A deep into the Caucasus. Here a
German anti-tank unit is silhouetted by
smoke from burning oilfields at Maikop, fired
by their defenders, in the last week of August.

RIGHT

Operation *Heron* saw Army Group B drive for the Volga with the aim of taking Stalingrad and extending down the river as far as Astrakhan. Here German infantry move up as Stalingrad burns on the horizon.

LEFT

The bitter fighting at Stalingrad placed overwhelming emphasis on the courage and determination of small groups of men fighting in what soon became a blighted landscape. Here a German machine-gun detachment – the empty ammunition boxes to its rear are evidence of heavy fighting – defends the ruins of suburban cottages.

ABOVE
A German infantry officer, whose decorations include the Iron Cross 1st Class and the infantry assault badge, issues orders. The soldier on the left has equipped himself with a captured Russian sub-machine gun.

LEFT
Street fighting in Stalingrad: Russians fire on a German-held block of flats.

LEFT
After the encirclement of Stalingrad Hitler gave Manstein command of the newly created Army Group Don and ordered him to break into the pocket. Here a German tank hits a Russian mine during an abortive counterattack, December 20.

BELOW
Friedrich Paulus, commander of 6th Army, was promoted to field-marshal on 30 January in Hitler's expectation that he would commit suicide rather than capitulate. However, he surrendered the following day. These Russian officers – the term was reintroduced by Stalin in 1942 – are still wearing collar rank badges, soon to be replaced by tsarist-style shoulder boards, all part of an attempt to restore the army's morale and efficiency.

ABOVE

The Germans lost some 200,000 men at Stalingrad: most of their prisoners of war did not survive captivity. Here a column of prisoners winds its way across the frozen steppe. Those in white fur hats are Romanians: defeat at Stalingrad struck a chill into Germany's allies.

RIGHT

Stalingrad was not an isolated setback: these young Germans were captured by a Russian offensive in the middle Don.

NORTH AFRICA

In 1942 Allied fortunes in North Africa ebbed at first, when Rommel turned the strong defensive line running from Gazala on the coast to Bir Hacheim in the desert, took Tobruk and went on to cross the Egyptian frontier. There he was checked, initially at First Alamein on July 1, and then at Alam Halfa at the very end of September. In October, Montgomery, the newly appointed commander of 8th Army, won the battle of El Alamein. The following month an Allied army landed in French North Africa, catching Axis forces in the theatre in a gigantic pincer which would eventually snap shut in 1943.

ABOVE
East meets west: the photographer Cecil Beaton catches an Egyptian girl admiring a poster of the actress Hedy Lamarr.

LEFT
A Hudson MkVI bomber over the Pyramids, Summer 1942.

RIGHT
A January 1942 photograph of an Italian convoy caught by the RAF on the coast road during Rommel's withdrawal the previous month.

ABOVE

Although this photograph is blurred and undated (though it passed the censor in 1942) it gives a good impression of infantry of 4th Indian Division moving up with a shell bursting dangerously close.

RIGHT

The British might have won the Gazala battles of May–June 1942, but superior German generalship and all-arms tactics eventually proved too much for them. But the Germans did not have it all their own way. Here a new US-supplied Grant tank, which mounted a 75mm gun in its hull and a 37mm in the turret, passes a burning German tank.

LEFT
A 25-pdr in action at night, June 2. These weapons were often used in the anti-tank role in the desert, and during the Gazala battles their detachments frequently fought them to a finish as German tanks overran their positions.

RIGHT
The Stuka dive-bomber, so useful for providing close air support, was very vulnerable without fighter support. These Messerschmitt Me 109 fighters aircraft wait at their desert strip while ground crew snatch an alfresco lunch.

RIGHT

The fall of Tobruk on June 21, was a heavy blow to Churchill. Here the first German vehicle to enter the town pauses in front of abandoned vehicles and a sign, couched in Tommy's humour, pointing to a barber shop.

BELOW

By September 1941 there were nearly 60,000 South African troops in Egypt, 15,000 of them black: all had volunteered to serve outside South Africa, and wore an orange strip on their epaulettes to mark the fact. 1st South African Division was bloodily engaged during Operation *Crusader*, and the over 10,000 South Africans were captured when Tobruk fell. These South Africans take cover while their truck is bombed, June 4, 1942.

ABOVE
German tanks roll eastwards following
British withdrawal from Gazala.

RIGHT
One of a series of photographs taken in
July, just after Rommel had been checked at
"First Alamein", showing British guardsmen
practising an advance with tanks. At this
juncture the "brave but baffled" 8th Army
was holding a strong position just west
of the little railway halt of El Alamein,
but it did not fully find its feet until the
arrival of Montgomery in mid-August.

FOLLOWING PAGES
A British 6-pdr anti-tank
gun in action, August 11.

Montgomery preferred to let metal,
not flesh, do the business of battle.
On the night of 23–4 October, 882
guns pounded the Axis defences before
his men began to break into them.

German reinforcements moving up by
train to the El Alamein front in October.

ABOVE
British infantry advance in open order
on October 24. The infantry was tasked
with "crumbling" Rommel's defences.

An Advanced Dressing Station, October 24.
An officer of the Royal Army Medical
Corps gives a drink to one of the wounded.

ABOVE
German prisoners await transport at
El Alamein corner, October 25.
Some 30,000 prisoners of war were taken.

General von Thoma, commander
of the Afrika Korps (now an elite
minority in the larger German–Italian
force in North Africa) introduced to
Montgomery after capture, November 4.

Crusader cruiser tanks in
pursuit after Alamein.

Cecil Beaton's view of the crew of a
Martin Maryland light bomber receiving
a last-minute briefing before take-off.
Slick co-operation between ground and
air forces characterized Montgomery's
conduct of the battle in North Africa.

ESCAPE OF THE SCHARNHORST

Early in 1941 the battlecruisers *Scharnhorst* and *Gneisenau* broke
out into the Atlantic and sank 22 merchantmen before entering
the French port of Brest, where they were damaged by bombing.
In 1942 Hitler, who feared an Allied invasion of Norway, ordered
them to sail through the Channel with the heavy cruiser *Prinz
Eugen*, which had accompanied the ill-fated *Bismarck*. Although
the British had warning of Operation *Cerberus* through ULTRA
intelligence and had plans to deal with it, a combination of
German skill, British fumbling and sheer mischance enabled
the Germans to complete the Channel dash in the face of brave
but piecemeal attacks on February 11–12, 1942.

ABOVE

Scharnhorst and *Gneisenau* were damaged
by mines on the Channel dash and required
extensive repair. *Scharnhorst* eventually
reached Norway, but was sunk in
December 1943. *Gneisenau*, crippled by
bombing in dry dock, never fought again.

BRITAIN AT WAR

Britain was emphatically a nation at war. Food rationing began in January 1940, and that autumn saw the beginning of the London blitz, with endemic air raids thereafter. A 1940 extension of the 1939 Emergency Powers Act gave the government "complete control over ...all persons, rich and poor ... and all property." Britain mobilized a higher proportion of its population than any other combatant: by June 1944 22% of the working population was in the services and another 33% in war work. Women replaced men in factories, public transport and on the land. Men were not only drafted into the forces, but eventually down the mines as well.

ABOVE

Mrs Minnie Murless of the Wynnstay guest house clips the ration books of her guests. There were weekly forms for butcher and grocer, and every two month the local Food Office required detailed lists of consumption. Fuel and animal food required separate permits.

BELOW

"Local defence," reads the original caption, "releases men for overseas offence." Like most Home Guard units, this one includes those too old or too young for regular service as well as men in some key occupations which spared them regular call-up.

Rail travel was cramped and uncertain. Here a member of the WAAF (Women's Auxiliary Air Force) and a soldier sit on their luggage in the corridor of a London to Scotland express.

BELOW

Crewe station in the small hours of the morning. A Royal Navy petty officer and his family on their way from Northern Ireland await their connection.

In May 1942 Molotov, the Soviet Commissar for Foreign Affairs, flew to England to sign a Treaty of Alliance and Mutual Assistance. Here he is walking next to Churchill in the garden of No 10 Downing Street. Clement Attlee, Deputy Prime Minister, is shrouded in tobacco smoke in the centre of the photograph, and Anthony Eden, Foreign Secretary, is just behind Churchill.

Russian ambassador Ivan Maisky accepts the first tank produced under the "Tanks for Russia" scheme. War material was shipped to Russia, often at great cost, in the arctic convoys through the Norwegian and Barents seas.

ABOVE

Members of the Women's Land Army ploughing in Hertfordshire, March 1942.

RIGHT

Between January 1942 and D-Day in 1944 more than a million and a half US servicemen arrived in Britain. There were complaints that the Americans were "overpaid, oversexed and over here", but paradoxically most civilians were sympathetic to black GIs, victims of colour bars in their own army.

OPPOSITE PAGE

Although women did not fly in direct combat, 166 served in the Air Transport Auxiliary which ferried aircraft from factories to their bases, and servicewomen like this Wren (from WRNS, Women's Royal Naval Service) radio mechanic flew to test radios.

LEFT
In 1942 the Germans mounted hit and run "Baedeker raids" on historic cities in retaliation for raids on Lübeck and Rostock. Canterbury cathedral was damaged in June.

ABOVE
Many anti-aircraft batteries has male and female personnel. These women of the ATS (Auxiliary Territorial Service) operate a mobile power-plant on an anti-aircraft site in December 1942.

RAID ON DIEPPE

On August 19, 1942, the British mounted Operation *Jubilee*, a large-scale raid on the port of Dieppe. Some 4,900 Canadian, 1,000 British and 50 US troops left five English ports in a fleet of 237 warships and landing craft. Air support was inadequate and intelligence poor, and despite some minor successes the main assault was a bloody failure, with 3,367 Canadian casualties. The Royal Navy lost a destroyer and several landing craft, and the RAF 106 aircraft to only 48 German. Although useful lessons were learnt from Dieppe, the operation's unjustifiable risks were worsened by its labyrinthine planning.

BELOW
Landing craft run in towards the beach
under cover of floating smoke dischargers.

ABOVE
The frontal assault was mounted by
The Royal Hamilton Light Infantry and
The Essex Scottish, with armour from
the 14th Canadian Army Tank Regiment
(The Calgary Tanks), supported by the
Fusiliers Mont-Royal. Twelve tanks were
stopped on the beach because shingle
jammed their tracks, and the 15 that
made their way inland were soon knocked
out. Here a German infantryman picks
his way among blanketed Canadian dead.

RIGHT
Canadian prisoners are
marched through Dieppe.

ABOVE
Propagandists found some crumbs of comfort: No 4
Commando, seen here after returning to Newhaven,
had taken the Varengeville battery. The US Ranger
makes the point that this was the first time Americans had
been in action on the ground in Europe during the war.

GUADALCANAL

In mid-1942 the US Joint Chiefs of Staff authorized Operation *Watchtower*, an attack on Tulagi and Guadalcanal in the Solomon islands, where the Japanese had begun to construct an airfield. The initial American landing, carried out by 1st Marine Division, was successful, but the Japanese reacted swiftly, and both sides reinforced, leading to vicious fighting on land, in the air and at sea. The Americans completed the unfinished airfield on Guadalcanal (Henderson Field), and its possession gave them a decisive edge. In mid-November the three-day naval battle of Guadalcanal, a costly victory for the Americans, marked the climax of the struggle. Japanese survivors were evacuated in January 1943.

ABOVE
US Marines landing on Guadalcanal, August 7. Initial lack of opposition encouraged the caption to describe a "successful attack against the occupying Japanese."

RIGHT
In what became known as the battle of the Tenaru River in late August a 900-strong Japanese force was literally wiped out.

THE MALTA CONVOYS

The island of Malta possessed the only British-held harbour between Gibraltar and Alexandria and was crucial to convoys bringing supplies to forces in the Western desert. The Axis hoped to neutralize it by air attack, and Malta was besieged from 1940 till the Axis surrender in North Africa in May 1943. It owed its survival to fighter squadrons based on its airfields and fast convoys that ran the gauntlet to reach the island. In March–April 1942 Malta received twice the tonnage of bombs dropped on London during the Blitz, and in all 1,493 of her citizens were killed and 3,764 wounded.

OPPOSITE PAGE
The crew of a pom-pom multiple anti-aircraft gun aboard a destroyer escorting the *Pedestal* convoy enjoying a smoke break between air attacks. The photographer had already been sunk aboard the cruiser HMS *Manchester*, and transferred to a destroyer "with his camera intact."

ABOVE
The aircraft carrier HMS *Indomitable* almost hidden by near misses from air attack as she helps escort the vital *Pedestal* convoy to Malta, August 1942.

RIGHT
Tugs bustle round the American tanker *Ohio*, crippled but still full of fuel, as she enters Valetta harbour, August 1942.

STRATEGIC AIR OFFENSIVE

In 1942 the strategic bombing offensive against Germany was substantially increased. The 1941 Butt report, which showed just how inaccurate night bombing actually was, encouraged the introduction of area bombing of German cities. Sir Arthur Harris took over as Commander-in-Chief of the RAF's Bomber Command in February. He quickly ordered fire-storm raids on Rostock and Lübeck, and then, in May, mobilized his second line and training aircraft to mount the first thousand-bomber raid, on Cologne.

OPPOSITE PAGE
RAF armourers fusing bombs prior to loading them aboard a Short Stirling at RAF Waterbeach, near Cambridge, April 30, 1942.

BELOW
The caption to this German photograph of the gutted Lübeck cathedral described the raid on the city as "a new crime against civilization." It helped inspire the German Baedeker raids, so called because the official announcing them declared that the Germans would attack all building marked with three stars in the Baedeker guidebook.

ABOVE
On the night of May 30, the first thousand
bomber raid was launched on Cologne. The
top picture shows a rubber factory at Deutz,
on the east bank of the Rhine, before the raid,
and the lower picture shows it afterwards.

ABOVE
The four-engined Avro Lancaster came
into service in early 1942. Although it
was generally used at night, this
photograph shows a low-level
daylight raid on the Schneider armament
works at Le Creusot on October 17.

RIGHT
Another daylight attack, this by Lockheed Venturas, Douglas Bostons and de Havilland Mosquitos on the Philips radio valve works in the Dutch town of Eindhoven, December 6.

BELOW
German flak and fighters imposed a steady toll on bombers. Here a Vickers Wellington of the Polish 301 (Pomeranian) Squadron, lies in the mud of a Dutch estuary.

OPERATION TORCH

Operation *Torch*, the Allied invasion of French North Africa, was launched in November under the command was the unknown US Lieutenant General Dwight D. Eisenhower. The Allies tried to ensure French co-operation, and in the event resistance was patchy in quality and quantity. Fortuitously, Admiral Darlan, Marshal Petain's deputy, was visiting his sick son in Algiers, and was persuaded to order a ceasefire. The Germans swiftly sent troops to Tunisia, and the Allied advance bogged down with the rains of early winter.

ABOVE
Although the Vichy government repudiated Darlan's ceasefire, Hitler was furious and invaded the Unoccupied Zone of France. A German force had orders to seize the French fleet at Toulon, but the French activated a well-prepared plan and the fleet was scuttled by its crews in the nick of time. Here damaged and sunk cruisers and destroyers can be seen through the smoke of burning heavy cruisers.

ABOVE
With Allied convoys at sea, sailors
could be told their destination.
Here Rear Admiral Sir Harold Burrough
explains forthcoming operations
to officers and men aboard his flagship.

OPPOSITE PAGE
American troops, part of the Central Task
Force, on their way ashore by landing
craft at Oran. It was thought that the
French would be less likely to engage
the Americans than the British, still
mistrusted because of the attack on
Mers-el-Kebir and the fighting in the Levant.

1943

THE ALLIES GAIN MOMENTUM

ALTHOUGH THE TIDE OF WAR HAD TURNED IN 1942, 1943 WAS TO SHOW THAT AXIS FORTUNES WOULD EBB NEITHER SWIFTLY NOR EVENLY. IN NORTH AFRICA THE GERMANS COUNTERATTACKED SHARPLY AT THE KASSERINE PASS IN FEBRUARY AND AT MEDENINE THE FOLLOWING MONTH BEFORE BEING FORCED TO SURRENDER IN MID-MAY.

THE ALLIES WENT ON TO SICILY and thence to Italy, where hopes of a quick victory foundered – as such hopes so often do – in the face of an intransigent enemy and harsh terrain. On the Eastern Front the Russians made good progress after Stalingrad, but Field Marshal Erich von Manstein sprung a masterly counterstroke at Kharkov before the failure of the German offensive at Kursk in July left the balance of power tilted firmly in Russia's favour. The Americans continued their advance across the Pacific, but it was all too evident that the Japanese would fight to the bitter end for even the tiniest island. In Burma the picture remained bleak, although news of the first Chindit operation behind Japanese lines was a useful fillip to morale. The strategic bombing offensive gained weight as the year wore on, while in the Atlantic the Allies at last gained the edge over German submarines: a decisive victory in an otherwise inconclusive year.

The Germans had responded to Allied landings in North Africa in November 1942 by rapidly reinforcing their forces in Tunisia – initially Colonel General von Arnim's 5th Panzer Army. Arnim played his cards with skill, blunting the attack by Lieutenant General Kenneth Anderson's 1st Army and going on to mount a counterattack. Rommel, meanwhile, had fallen back from Libya into south-eastern Tunisia before the advance of Montgomery's 8th Army, and added his own weight to the counteroffensive, striking hard at the Americans in the Kasserine Pass. Indeed, had Arnim and Rommel got on better, or had their efforts been better co-ordinated by Italian Commando Supremo, they might have done very serious damage to the Allies in Tunisia. As it was, Rommel was ordered north, straight towards Allied reinforcements, and called off his attack on February 22.

Both sides reorganized. Rommel took command of the newly formed Army Group Africa, with his German–Italian Panzer Army becoming First Italian Army. While the fighting at Kasserine was in progress the Allies instituted a unified command in the theatre, with Eisenhower as Commander-in-Chief working through General Sir Harold Alexander as commander of 18th Army Group combining 1st and 8th Armies. Air Chief Marshal Sir Arthur Tedder became Commander-in-Chief of Mediterranean Air Command. The advantage bestowed by ULTRA was demonstrated, yet again, when radio intercepts revealed that Rommel was planning to use all three of his panzer divisions against the 8th Army at Medenine, enabling Montgomery to set up an anti-tank screen to meet them. In early March Rommel departed for Europe, leaving Arnim to command Army Group Africa. Later that month Montgomery was checked in a frontal attack on the Mareth Line, north-west of Medenine, but hooked around its inland flank. By now Army Group Africa was in growing difficulties, starved of supplies by Allied air and naval blockade and compressed between 1st and 8th Armies. Alexander's final offensive began on April 22, and although Arnim's men fought hard the issue was never seriously in doubt: the last Axis forces surrendered on May 13. The Allies had suffered 76,000 casualties, and took more than 238,000 prisoners.

Churchill and Roosevelt met at Casablanca in January in a conference that affirmed the Allied policy of dealing with Germany first and established Sicily as the next objective in the Mediterranean. Operation *Husky*, the invasion of Sicily, was mounted by Alexander's 15th Army Group, comprising Montgomery's 8th Army and Lieutenant General George S. Patton's

7th US Army. It began on July 10, and the airborne element of the operation went badly wrong, with many gliders landing in the sea. Inter-Allied friction did not improve matters, and although Patton took Palermo on July 22, progress was slow. General Alfredo Guzzioni was in overall command of Axis forces, but in practice General Hans Hube of 14th Panzer Corps conducted a skilful defence. The Allies were unable to prevent a well-conducted evacuation which began on the night of August 11–12. An American patrol entered Messina on August 16, and the last of Hube's men slipped away that night.

For all its flaws, the Sicilian campaign had at least one useful result. Italy's enthusiasm for the war had been cooling for some time, and both American entry into the war and the Red Army's successes in 1942 helped change the popular mood. On the one hand a long tradition of emigration had created a respect for American power, and on the other the Italian Communist party had rebuilt its structure and was strengthening its appeal. Mussolini's position was undermined as both industrialists and fascist leaders began to favour a separate peace; opposition coalesced around King Victor Emmanuel, and Mussolini's own grip on events became dangerously weak. On July 25, he was arrested, and Marshal Pietro Badoglio formed a government that began clandestine negotiations with the Allies and signed an outline armistice on September 3. There were attempts to take advantage of this, with a plan to send an airborne division to Rome, but in the event, nothing came of them. The Allies landed unopposed at Reggio di Calabria, across the straits of Messina, on September 3 and on September 9, mounted a full-scale landing at Salerno. The armistice was announced that day, but the Germans were prepared for it, and although there was some resistance (on the Greek island of Cephalonia an Italian division fought heroically: 4,750 survivors were shot after capture) the bulk of the Italian army was neutralized. The Germans sharply counter-attacked at Salerno, and their partial success encouraged Hitler to back Field Marshal Albert Kesselring, the talented Luftwaffe officer serving as Commander-in-Chief South-West, who favoured the inch-by-inch defence of Italy. The Germans constructed a series of defensive lines running across Italy, whose terrain – with the central mountain spine of the Apennines, from which rivers ran to the

Tyrrenian and Adriatic Seas – presented the Allies with a gruelling slog across rivers and mountains. As the year neared its close even Montgomery was sceptical. "I don't think we can get any spectacular results," he told Alan Brooke, Chief of the Imperial General Staff, "so long as it goes on raining: the whole country becomes a sea of mud and nothing on wheels can move off the roads." There remained substantial doubts about the strategic merits of the Italian campaign, especially with the invasion of Europe – which would have first call on men and equipment – scheduled for 1944.

On the Eastern Front the year began with the German surrender at Stalingrad and Russian exploitation that saw Kharkov, the main administrative and railway centre in the eastern Ukraine, recaptured in mid-February. However, Manstein, one of the war's most capable practitioners of armoured manoeuvre, counter-attacked "on the backhand", jabbing up into the flank and rear of the victorious Russians to recapture the town. The winter's campaign left a salient bulging into German lines round the railway junction of Kursk, between Belgorod and Orel. Hitler ordered Kluge (Army Group Centre) and Manstein (Army Group South) to prepare Operation *Citadel* to nip out the salient. The Russians, meanwhile, prepared formidable defences around Kursk, and when the Germans at last attacked on June 5, they did not make their usual progress. Although the 4th Panzer Army cut deep into the Russian position from the south, the 9th Army, attacking from the north, made less substantial gains: not only was Kursk an impossible goal, but Russian counterattacks saw fierce fighting which left German armour badly worn down. With some 1,300 tanks engaged, the fighting around Prokhorovka, in the south, became the largest armoured mêlée of the war. Hitler had long entertained doubts about the offensive, telling Guderian: "Whenever I think of this attack my stomach turns over." News of Allied landings in Sicily persuaded Hitler to close down the operation in order to free troops for transfer to the south, and the initiative passed to the Russians. At first Field Marshal Walter Model held his ground, but as more German divisions were shifted to Italy cohesive defence became more difficult, and in August the Russians developed a series of parallel thrusts towards the River

Dnieper, wresting large bridgeheads on the west bank. When Stalin met Churchill and Roosevelt at Tehran in November it was as supreme commander of forces which were emphatically winning.

The Casablanca conference in January had reaffirmed the principle of "Germany First", and the Americans decided to use thirty per cent of their resources against Japan. Strategy for the Pacific War was fleshed out in the months that followed. MacArthur and Halsey were to continue their advance along the coast of New Guinea and through the Solomon Isles towards the Philippines, while in the eastern Pacific, Nimitz would move from the Gilberts to the Marshalls and on to the Palaus. It took Halsey a month to take New Georgia, and the hard fighting there induced him to bypass Kolombangara to seize the lightly held Vella Lavella in mid-August, establishing a technique which was to prove useful thereafter. By the year's end US forces had landed on Bougainville and New Britain, and, having reversed an earlier decision to invade the strongly held Rabual, at the eastern end of New Britain, now pounded it repeatedly from air and sea.

Nimitz's attack took longer to come, and it began with an attack on Tarawa in the Gilberts on November 20. Despite a ferocious bombardment by Vice-Admiral Spruance's 5th Fleet, the Japanese garrison fought back savagely. Armoured amphibians, used here for the first time, proved very successful, but marines lost heavily as landing craft carrying follow-up troops grounded on coral reefs. The tiny island, no bigger that New York's Central Park, took three days to clear and cost over a thousand US dead and twice as many wounded. Although these losses caused grave concern in the USA, the battle provided American commanders with useful information on the conduct of amphibious assaults, and, with tactics refined, they prepared to push on into the Marshall Islands in early 1944.

In Burma, however, Japanese fortunes seemed more assured. Both sides reorganized their command structure in 1943, with the Japanese creating the Burma Area Army under Lieutenant General Kawabe Masukazu in March, and the Allies establishing South-East Asia Command (SEAC) under Admiral Lord Louis Mountbatten in September. The British launched an unsuccessful offensive down the Arakan coast in an effort, to take Akyab and its airfields, but were badly mauled by the Japanese. On a more optimistic note, Brigadier Orde Wingate, an unconventional soldier with experience of irregular warfare in both Palestine and Ethiopia, led a long-range penetration by a brigade-sized force of Chindits – so called from the *chinthe*, the protective lion at the entrance to Burmese temples. Although the operation did little material damage, and cost the lives of about a third of the 3,000 participants, news of the achievements of "ordinary family men from Liverpool and Manchester" was well-received in Britain, and in Burma it did much to dispel the image of the Japanese as supermen and invincible jungle fighters. Wingate himself, taken up by an enthusiastic Churchill, brought "a whiff of the jungle" to the Quebec conference in August, and was instrumental in persuading the Americans to agree to an Anglo–American operation, on a much larger scale, the following year.

Although Allied victory in the Battle of the Atlantic was less obvious than events in Tunisia, Sicily or the Pacific it was actually more significant, for without it there could have been no American build-up in Britain and no invasion of France. A combination of factors produced the crisis of early 1943. The need to find escorts for convoys to North Africa led to the concentration of convoys across the North Atlantic at the very time that U-boat "wolf packs" gathered to attack them. Although ULTRA and improved anti-submarine technology helped the Allies, in March, when ULTRA briefly lost the thread once more, all North Atlantic convoys were found by the Germans: half were attacked and nearly a quarter of their shipping was sunk. However, in mid-March ULTRA re-penetrated German communications, and Allied naval resources were concentrated on bringing the submarines to battle. Large support groups, one with an aircraft carrier, buttressed convoy escorts; more carriers arrived, and in May the long-range Liberator aircraft at last closed the Atlantic gap. The Germans lost almost 100 submarines in the first five months of the year, half of them in May. Shipping losses dropped dramatically, and US shipyards were now building at a rate that comfortably outstripped them. Not only was Britain safe from starvation, but the American build-up of men and equipment gained the momentum which was to reach fruition in 1944.

NORTH AFRICA

The North African campaign had a sting in its tail. In January Arnim mounted an offensive, catching ill-equipped French divisions off guard and going on to shake the Americans. Rommel, forced steadily westwards by Montgomery's advance, put in an attack of his own, inflicting a sharp defeat on the Americans at the Kasserine Pass in February. The Allies then reorganized their chain of command, forming the 18th Army Group, comprising both armies (Anderson's 1st and Montgomery's 8th) fighting in Tunisia. Axis forces were gradually compressed into a pocket round Tunis, and the last of them surrendered in mid-May, leaving 238,000 prisoners in Allied hands.

BELOW
The Mareth Line, based on prewar French defences in southern Tunisia, was held by Rommel's old army, now renamed the 1st Italian army under General Giovanni Messe. Montgomery's first attack, on March 19, failed, but a hook round the desert flank forced Messe to pull back. Here a 4.5-inch medium gun bombards the line.

LEFT
On March 6, Rommel turned on
Montgomery at Medenine, but,
using information from ULTRA,
Montgomery was ready for him
and the attack was easily repulsed.
These Gurkhas are using their distinctive
weapon, the kukri, near Medenine,
but this shot comes from a sequence that
suggests that it was staged for the camera.

RIGHT
This, in contrast, is a real photograph
of the Medenine battle, showing a German
Mk III Special knocked out by 73rd
Anti-Tank Regiment Royal Artillery,
part of the anti-tank screen deployed
by Montgomery as a result of ULTRA.

ABOVE

The end in Tunisia. An American intelligence officer interrogates two prisoners. Two French soldiers, once more on the Allied side, are in the background.

LEFT

Roosevelt, in North Africa for the Casablanca conference, took the opportunity to visit troops in the field, the first President since Lincoln to do so.

THE BATTLE OF THE CONVOYS

Churchill wrote that the only thing that really worried him was the submarine menace. The Battle of the Atlantic reached its crescendo in 1943, when operations in North Africa drew escorts away from the Atlantic, and Britain depended utterly on the main North Atlantic convoy routes at the very time that German submarines, concentrated in "wolf packs", redoubled their efforts, paying particular attention to the narrowing gap in mid-Atlantic left uncovered by land-based aircraft. ULTRA proved decisive, enabling escorts to find submarines with accuracy: the Germans lost 47 in May alone. Sinkings continued, but the battle was won by the end of the month.

RIGHT

The *Torch* convoy at sea, November 1942. The convoy was kept under an air umbrella that reduced the risk of attack, but demands imposed on convoy escorts by the demands of North Africa were to influence the Battle of the Atlantic.

BELOW

Arctic convoys ferried supplies to Russia. Here the cruiser HMS *Belfast* is at sea in northern waters March 1943.

RIGHT
Most British warships relied on multi-barrelled automatic "pom-poms" for close defence against aircraft. This air spotter, binoculars at the ready, watches for hostile aircraft.

LEFT
The cruiser HMS *Sheffield*, on the same convoy as *Belfast* (*previous page*), has both forward turrets trained to the beam to avoid damage to their canvas blast screens. Nevertheless, one turret roof was torn right off by a wave.

OPPOSITE PAGE
Depth-charges dropped by a Canadian corvette. The Canadians, short of modern equipment and adequate destroyers, had a particularly hard war in the Atlantic.

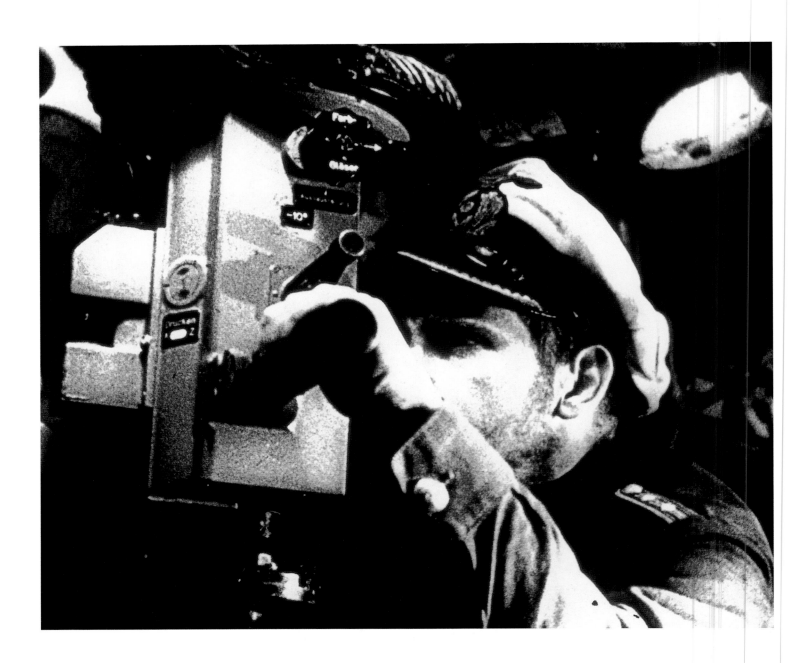

ABOVE

A U-Boat commander at his periscope.
German submarine crews had a horrifyingly
high casualty rate: 40,900 men served
in submarines during the war, and
28,000 perished. Admiral Dönitz,
Commander-in-Chief of the German navy,
lost both his sailor sons, one in a submarine.

LEFT

In 1943 the German introduced two types of anti-shipping glider bomb. This photograph shows a near miss on a freighter by a glider-bomb launched by a Heinkel He 177.

RIGHT

The last moments of a freighter, seen from a submarine. From January to May 1943 Allied shipping loses averaged 450,000 tons per month.

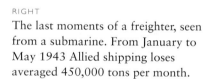

LEFT

U625 sinking after depth-charge attack by a Sunderland of 422 Squadron, Royal Canadian Air Force, 10 March 1944.

ABOVE
This U-Boat, attacked at periscope
depth by a Sunderland, was brought to
the surface by depth charges and then sunk.

ABOVE
Merchant seamen scramble
aboard a US Coastguard cutter.

FOLLOWING PAGES
Firemen "Bonny" Bartell and "Snowy" Foster, both
of Canning Town in East London, come up for a
breather on a North African Convoy, July 1943.

KATYN

When Poland was divided between Russia and Germany in 1939 over 180,000 Polish prisoners of war fell into Soviet hands: officers were segregated in special camps. In April 1943, the Germans discovered a mass grave in Katyn forest near Smolensk, later found to contain the remains of 4,400 Polish officers, and accused the Russians of mass murder, summoning an international team of experts to investigate the crime. Although the Russians long blamed the Germans for the atrocity, in 1990 they at last admitted responsibility.

The victims had their hands wired behind their backs and had been shot in the back of the head. This evocative photograph sums up the fate of tens of thousands of victims of mass murder during the war.

The German-sponsored international experts (all but one from Axis or occupied countries) examining of the bodies of Katyn. When the London-based Polish government in exile suggested an impartial International Red Cross investigation, the Russians broke off diplomatic relations.

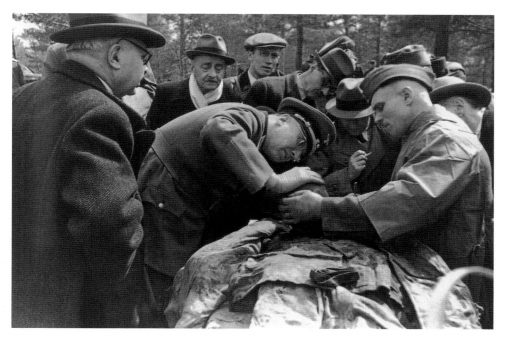

THE PACIFIC WAR

In early 1943 Australian troops, fighting in dreadful conditions, extinguished the Japanese beachheads of Buna, Gona and Sanananda Point on New Guinea. The Casablanca conference that January suggested that one-third of Allied resources should be deployed against Japan, but the British felt unable to agree to a fixed formula. The US Joint Chiefs agreed a broad strategy, with MacArthur and Admiral William F. Halsey pushing on through the Solomons and along the New Guinea coast, while Nimitz "island hopped" across the central Pacific towards Japan.

OPPOSITE PAGE

An Australian forward post near Sanananda, less than thirty yards from the Japanese. The robust and reliable .303 Bren was the light automatic weapon in British and Commonwealth infantry sections.

BELOW

Australian infantry, assisted by a Stuart light tank, during the final assault on Buna.

ABOVE
The battle for Buna sorely tried the US 32nd
Infantry Division, which had not been trained
for jungle warfare and was poorly equipped:
it lost almost ninety per cent of its strength as
battle casualties and sick. But it was a
disaster for the Japanese: this photograph
shows Japanese bodies on the shoreline.

Japanese prisoners were very rare. These, both badly wounded, were taken when Gona fell.

After expelling the Japanese from southern New Guinea the Australians moved northwards. In September 1943 the Japanese strongholds of Lae and Salamua were taken. Here US paratroops jump into the Markham Valley in an effort to block the Japanese escape from Lae.

ABOVE

New Zealanders had already played a distinguished part in the war in the Western Desert, and added to these laurels in the Pacific. Here New Zealand troops (in their distinctive "lemon-squeezer" hats) land from US landing craft on Vella Lavella in the Solomons.

LEFT

Rabual, on the island of New Britain, was a powerful Japanese air base. It was so heavily defended that a decision to capture it was reversed at the Quebec conference in August 1943, and it was so badly hammered from air and sea that the Japanese substantially scaled it down. Here a US aircraft attacks with a white phosphorus incendiary bomb.

BELOW

On November 1, 1943, the Americans landed on Bougainville, strategically placed between MacArthur's and Nimitz's areas of operations. The Japanese held a tiny part of the island to the very end of the war, but most of their positions had been taken in this sort of knock-down drag-out fighting: a flame thrower scorches a Japanese bunker while riflemen give covering fire.

Almost all Japanese preferred
suicide to surrender. These infantrymen
on Tarawa have shot themselves in
the head, using a toe to pull the trigger.

This essence of the war at sea: a Japanese
torpedo-bomber is hit by short-range fire
from a US carrier, December 4, 1943.

DAMBUSTERS

617 Squadron RAF was formed in March 1943 to attack the
Möhne and Sorpe dams, which provided water to the Ruhr,
and the Eder, which helped keep canals at navigable depth.
A special bomb was developed for the mission by Barnes Wallis.
Dropped from low level, it bounced on the water before sliding
down the dam wall. On the night of May 16–17, the Möhne and
Eder dams were both breached, but although loss of life and
industrial dislocation were considerable, the damage was short-lived.

BELOW
Wing Commander Guy Gibson, commander
of 617 Squadron, boarding his Lancaster.
Eight of the nineteen bombers were lost.

LEFT
The Barnes Wallis 9,250 lb (4,195 kg) bouncing bomb slung below a Lancaster.

BELOW
The breached Möhne dam four hours after the raid.

FOLLOWING PAGE
Guy Gibson, photographed near RAF Scampton on July 22 1943. Awarded the Victoria Cross, Britain's highest award for military valour, Gibson was killed the following year at the age of 26.

ALLIED CONFERENCES

There were twelve major Allied conferences during the war, but it was only at two – Tehran in 1943 and Yalta in 1945 – that Churchill, Roosevelt and Stalin were all present. There were three conferences in 1943, at Casablanca ("Symbol") in January, Quebec ("Quadrant") in August and at Tehran ("Eureka") in November and December.

ABOVE
Churchill and Roosevelt meet the press at Casablanca. The conference affirmed the policy of "Germany first", identified Sicily as the next Allied objective, and saw the first use of the term "Unconditional Surrender."

LEFT
The shape of postwar Europe was discussed at Tehran, reflecting Soviet fears of a future German resurgence. The Stalingrad sword, a gift from King George VI to the people of Stalingrad, was presented during the conference: here Marshal Voroshilov shows the sword to Roosevelt while Stalin and Churchill (the latter dressed as an air commodore) look on.

THE SICILIAN CAMPAIGN

Operation *Husky*, the invasion of Sicily, sought to weaken the
German army, make the Mediterranean safe for Allied shipping and
put pressure on Italy in the hope of driving her out of the war.
Eisenhower was in command, and Alexander's 15th Army Group
included Lieutenant General George S. Patton's US 7th Army and
Montgomery's British 8th. Amphibious and airborne landings began
on July 9–10, and although the latter fared badly (with the war's
worst friendly fire incident when transport aircraft overflew the Allied
fleet) the operation was a success, although it went more slowly than
had been hoped. Axis forces were slickly evacuated in mid-August.

ABOVE
US troops landing near Licata
on July 10. The night landings were
hampered by high winds and a heavy swell.

RIGHT
A British Bren-gun carrier (an open-topped
light armoured vehicle with a variety of
uses) coming ashore in Sicily.

FOLLOWING PAGES
A US Sherman tank rolling into
Palermo, July 26. Bedsheets and white
flags denote what the original caption
calls "surrender and a welcome peace."

ABOVE
Many American soldiers had Sicilian
or Italian roots. Here Corporal Salvatore
di Marco, in the rear of the jeep, is
re-united with former friends and
neighbours, in Messojuso, August 11.

ABOVE

Men of 6th Battalion The Royal Innsikilling
Fusiliers house-clearing in the Sicilian town
of Centuripe. There was sharp fighting
in the campaign, which cost the Allies
some 7,000 killed and 15,000 wounded.

RIGHT

A damaged sign points to Messina, site
of the ferry crossing to the mainland.
The mutilated portrait of Mussolini
underlines a shift in the balance of power
in Italy: on July 25, King Victor Emmanuel
III had placed Mussolini under arrest.

RIGHT

Children playing in a badly
bombed street in Sicily.

BELOW

A British officer samples local colour.
Although photographs such as this
had their merits, they radiated a false
impression and contributed to the slur
that troops in Italy were "D-Day Dodgers."

ABOVE
Two wounded soldiers of the 8th Army
at a field dressing station in Sicily.

RIGHT
An officer of the Intelligence Corps
questions a civilian at Trecastagni, Sicily.

THE STRATEGIC AIR OFFENSIVE

American bombers had begun operating from British bases in 1942, and the Combined Bomber Offensive was approved at the Casablanca conference. The RAF's Bomber Command generally operated by night to reduce losses, and the Americans, reaching out beyond the range of fighter cover and bombing by day at first suffered very heavy losses. Rather than switch to night bombing, they worked on extending the range of their fighters. In mid-1943 the Thunderbolt could escort bombers to the Ruhr; in November the Lightning could reach Berlin, and by December 1944 the Mustang could cover most of Germany.

ABOVE
The Avro Lancaster S for Sugar made her 97th operational flight over Germany in May 1944. She is seen here being loaded with 4000 lb and 500 lb bombs prior to her 97th operation, as part of an Australian squadron.

ABOVE
Four Lancaster bombers seen under
the prop wing of another Lancaster.

ABOVE

In a scene whose splashes of light make
it somehow reminiscent of Rembrandt's
Night Watch the crew of a returning
bomber, mugs of cocoa to hand, are
debriefed by an intelligence officer.

OPPOSITE PAGE
A Lancaster over Hamburg on the night of January 30, 1943, silhouetted against the glow of fires and the bright smears of flak.

ABOVE
The Americans initially championed the concept of the self-defending bomber. This B-17G carried thirteen .5-inch machine guns: here the right waist-gunner scans the sky for German fighters. However, 1943 demonstrated that even these Flying Fortresses needed fighter escort if they were to survive in daylight over Germany.

FOLLOWING PAGES
B-17s of the US Army Air Force's 8th Air Force over Germany in mid-1943. Above them are the criss-crossed vapour trails of the escorting fighters.

ABOVE

Three P-51D Mustangs of 361st
Fighter Group with an older P-51B in
the background. With auxiliary drop
tanks for fuel under each wing, the
Merlin-engined Mustangs could
eventually escort B-17 and B-24
bombers to Berlin and beyond.

ABOVE
Pilots of P47 Thunderbolt fighters which,
by the end of 1943, were making a real
difference to the air battle over Germany.

RIGHT

The port city of Hamburg was raided repeatedly. This photograph shows damage in July 1943: much worse was to come.

BELOW

An 88mm battery strikes back during an RAF raid. Heavy guns like this did not generally engage individual aircraft, but fired a barrage of shells fused to burst at the height of the incoming bomber stream.

ABOVE
Berlin, December 1943. Victims of a bombing raid are laid out for identification in a gymnasium decorated with Christmas trees. The strategic bomber offensive killed between 750,000 and a million Germans.

THE SURRENDER OF ITALY

After the fall of Mussolini Marshal Pietro Badoglio formed a government which clandestinely agreed an armistice with the Allies. The Allies landed in southern Italy on September 3, Italy's surrender was announced on the 8th and on the following day the Allies landed at Salerno, south of Naples. After narrowly beating off a vicious German counterattack the Allies pushed northwards, but the Germans defended the difficult ground from a series of well-prepared defensive lines and the campaign became a grim attritional slog.

BELOW

Badoglio (second left) after signing full armistice terms aboard HMS *Nelson* on September 29. Eisenhower is on his left: immediately behind them, from left to right, are Air Chief Marshal Tedder, Lieutenant General Mason-MacFarlane, and a nattily-dressed Alexander.

British troops coming ashore at Salerno
on September 9, from a landing craft
which is creating its own smoke screen.

A 3-inch mortar of 5th Battalion, The Hampshire Regiment in action during the fierce fighting for the Salerno beachhead.

ABOVE
In this apparently unposed shot, a PIAT (Projector Infantry Anti-Tank) of 2/6th Battalion, The Queen's Royal Regiment scores a direct hit on a German tank. The PIAT was a primitive spigot mortar which could throw a 3-lb shaped charge for about 100 yards.

The Germans pursued a rigorous
scorched earth policy: this device was
designed to rip up railway sleepers.

The first Allied convoy arrives in the
ruins of Naples harbour, with
Mount Vesuvius in the background,
October 4. There had been a popular
rising in the city, which the Germans sharply
repressed, just before the Allies appeared.

RIGHT
The Italian campaign was characterized by the need to cross numerous rivers which ran at right angles to the Allied advance. Here British troops cross the Volturno on October 13, on a bridge laid by US engineers.

LEFT
A Sherman tank of 8th Army towing a limber with an anti-tank gun moves down to the River Sangro with the Maiella mountains in the background, November 27.

The Monte Camino massif stands on the Bernhardt Line, held by the Germans in the winter of 1943. It was taken after bombardments that recalled the First World War. On December 2, 22,000 shells fell in a single hour.

In December 1, Canadian Infantry Division attacked Ortona on the Adriatic coast. The Germans were forced to withdraw after a week of severe house-to-house fighting. Tanks were used to "mousehole" walls to enable infantry to enter, and to deal with snipers.

THE EASTERN FRONT

After encircling Stalingrad the Russians mounted a general offensive
and retook Kharkov in mid-February. However, in a slick display
of manoeuvre Manstein counterattacked, routing the Russians
and recapturing Kharkov. These battles left a salient bulging into
the German lines around Kursk, between Belgorod and Orel, and
in July the Germans launched a major offensive to pinch it out.
The failure of this attack was followed by another Russian surge,
and although Manstein's skill helped prevent worse disasters by
the year's end the Russians had rolled the Germans right back
across the steppe, recapturing Smolensk and Kiev.

ABOVE
The Russians had ample time
to prepare their defences in the
Kursk salient, digging six belts of
three to five trench lines and laying vast
minefields to break up the German attack.

LEFT

The Battle of Kursk saw German armoured spearheads blunted by deep Russian defences before massive armoured counterattacks were unleashed. Kursk destroyed the last German armoured reserve in the east, and after it the initiative passed to the Russians.

BELOW

A German defensive position ploughed by Russian artillery: this "Red God of War" came increasingly to dominate the battlefield.

OPPOSITE PAGE

Disconsolate German prisoners, late 1943. Two in the front rank have lost their boots and face almost inevitable death.

ABOVE

The story of 1943: German troops falling back through a burning Russian town.

RIGHT

It was indeed a Great Patriotic War: Russian propagandists took trouble to portray the unity of the USSR's many national groups in the face of the German threat. Here the chairman of a collective farm in South Kazakhstan, with a benevolent Stalin looking on, makes a generous donation to the State War Loan.

THE SINKING OF THE SCHARNHORST

The 31,000 ton German battlecruiser *Scharnhorst* had escaped through the Channel with *Gneisenau* and the heavy cruiser *Prinz Eugen* in 1942. She was damaged by mines but, duly repaired, reached Norway in March 1943. On Christmas Day she sailed to attack an arctic convoy, but the British, acting on ULTRA intelligence, screened the convoy with a cruiser squadron which prevented *Scharnhorst* from reaching it. When she turned for home the was intercepted by Admiral Sir Bruce Fraser, Commander-in-Chief of the Home Fleet, and sunk on December 26.

ABOVE
Scharnhorst in heavy weather, 1942.

ABOVE
The battleship HMS *Duke of York*,
Admiral Fraser's flagship,
firing from her aft 14-inch turret.

ABOVE

Crippled by gunfire from *Duke of York*, *Scharnhorst* was torpedoed by the cruiser *Jamaica*, whose torpedomen pose for the camera. On the right is Petty Officer J. O. Mahoney of County Cork, whose presence underlines the contribution made to Britain's armed services by volunteers from neutral Eire.

FOLLOWING PAGES

Only 36 of *Scharnhorst*'s crew of over 2,000 survived. These survivors, dressed in kits supplied for rescued merchant seamen, were blindfolded for security as they landed. They were described as being (perhaps understandably) "lacking in surliness and arrogance" and thanked their rescuers with "three rousing cheers."

1944

THE WAR'S DYING FALL

BY 1944 THE WAR'S OUTCOME WAS SCARCELY IN DOUBT, BUT HOPES THAT IT WOULD ALL BY OVER IN CHRISTMAS PROVED MISPLACED. IN ITALY THE ALLIES CONTINUED THEIR LONG SLOG NORTHWARDS, TAKING ROME IN JUNE BUT FINDING MORE HILLS, RIVERS AND GERMANS BEHIND IT. IN BURMA THE DECISIVE BATTLES OF THE CAMPAIGN SAW THE JAPANESE TIDE BREAK AGAINST IMPHAL AND KOHIMA, AND IN THEIR WAKE THE ALLIES PUSHED SOUTH.

FURTHER EAST, the Japanese were in growing difficulties. Battles for islands like Saipan and Guam were bitter and bloody, but they brought the Americans inexorably closer to Japan, and island-based bombers struck ever harder at the home islands. On the Eastern Front the Russians won a series of victories, destroying Army Group Centre in June and July and standing braced, by the year's end, for the final offensive on the bomb-battered Reich. Finally, the western Allies had mounted their long-awaited invasion of France in June, and although it took them over two months to break out of Normandy, they then made impressive progress. A sting in the year's tail was provided by the last German offensive in the west, the "Battle of the Bulge."

In Italy, the most formidable of Kesselring's lines ran south of Rome. On its western flank, rivers had been stitched into a position buttressed by the massif of which Monte Cassino, towering above Cassino, formed the keystone. In January the US 36th Infantry Division was squandered trying to cross the Gari at Sant'Angelo, and the US 34th Infantry Division was fought to a standstill attempting to take Monte Cassino from the north. Further north, Lieutenant General Alponse Juin's French Expeditionary Corps, fighting with a determination that remains inadequately recognized by many Anglo–American historians, took the Colle Belvedere. In mid-February, in the second battle, the 2nd New Zealand Corps sent its 2nd New Zealand Division into the town while its 4th Indian Division attacked the high ground in the footsteps of the Americans. Gains were tiny, but the Benedictine monastery on Monte Cassino was wrecked by Allied bombers. It had not been

occupied, for the defending corps commander, Lieutenant General Fridolin von Senger und Etterlin, was not only a devout man, but recognized the monastery as a death-trap. The third battle began on March 15. This time the Indians attempted a frontal assault while the New Zealanders renewed their attack on the town, reduced to rubble by bombing. There were some gains, but the vital ground remained in the hands of the German parachutists who now held this sector.

For the fourth battle the Allies at last fought an army group operation, codenamed *Diadem*. Forces on the Adriatic coast were thinned out, enabling the 8th Army to take over the Cassino sector, while the 5th Army attacked further south, using the mountain-fighting skills of the French corps in the Aurunci mountains. This time the air plan was properly co-ordinated, and in Operation *Strangle* Allied aircraft concentrated on supply routes. The decisive blow was struck by 13th Corps, which crossed the Gari at Sant'Angelo: 1st Canadian Corps then exploited towards Rome and Monte Cassino was taken by 2nd Polish Corps.

The fighting at Cassino was complicated by the fact that on January 22, Major General John Lucas' 6th Corps of Mark Clark's 5th Army had landed at Anzio, just short of Rome. The operation, already shelved but revived on Churchill's insistence, lacked landing craft, and those assigned to it were required in England for the invasion of France. Lucas's force was too weak to take Rome and retain links with Anzio, and Lucas was given a last-minute warning by Clark not to stick his neck out.

The British–American landings were unopposed, and Lucas consolidated his position. By the time he was ready to advance the

Germans had cobbled together General Eberhard von Mackensen's 14th Army and the Allied advance was all but swamped by a ferocious counterattack. Yet again ULTRA proved vital in enabling the Allies to redeploy to meet new thrusts, but the fighting resembled episodes of the First World War. In February Lucas was replaced by Major General Lucian Truscott, and Kesselring acknowledged that he could not drive the Allies into the sea.

There was no breakout from Anzio until *Diadem*. Clark then cancelled Truscott's promising attack towards Route 6, up which the defenders of Cassino were withdrawing, in favour of a drive on Rome. Although the Eternal City fell to the Americans on June 4, too many of Cassino's defenders escaped to fight another day. Alexander's forces were weakened by sending troops to France, and although the Allies broke the Gothic Line (known to the Allies as the Pisa–Rimini Line) in September, the fighting largely died away in December.

In Burma, 1944 was the year when Allied fortunes changed. SEAC planned a three-pronged offensive. 15th Corps would advance down the Arakan and take Akyab; an American–Chinese force under Stilwell was to take Myitkyina, permitting the completion of the Ledo road from Assam to China; a second Chindit expedition, six brigades strong, would strike at Japanese lines of communication opposite Stilwell; finally, in the centre 4th Corps would push into northern Burma ready for a full-blown offensive. The Japanese intended not only to counterattack in the Arakan (*Ha-Go*), but to mount a more ambitious offensive (*U-Go*) towards India. Their plans misfired. In the Arakan the British stood fast, accepting encirclement and relying on air supply, and *U-Go*, launched in March, failed with huge cost before Imphal and Kohima. Stilwell took Myitkyina airfield in mid-May. The Chindits, who lost their leader in an air crash on March 24, cut some Japanese communications but did not have the effect expected of them. By the close of 1944 the Allies had begun to cross the Chindwin, were making good progress in the Arakan, and were about to reopen the land route with China.

In 1944, in a series of blows which testified to growing skill at the operational level of war, the Russians transformed the situation in the east. The siege of Leningrad was lifted in January; the Ukraine was cleared by March; the Crimea was recovered in April and Sevastopol in May, and in June and July Operation *Bagration* destroyed Army Group Centre. The Russians pushed on into Poland and the Baltic states. They took a bridgehead over the Vistula south of Warsaw, although, controversially, they were unable to break through to Warsaw in time to support the Poles of the Home Army, who rose on August 1. Romania and Bulgaria were knocked out of the Axis, even the Finns signed an armistice in September, and Budapest was encircled on December 26.

The western Allies had long planned to invade France, and the fact that the Germans were fettered to the Eastern Front did much to make their task feasible. The commanders for Operation *Overlord* were appointed in late 1943, but planning for the invasion had already been begun by the COSSAC team – "Chief of Staff to the Supreme Allied Commander (Designate)". The COSSAC staff had considered three options: the Pas de Calais; the bay of the Seine, and the Brittany coast. They selected the second option, and planned a three-division amphibious assault, its flanks secured by airborne drops. Montgomery, land force commander under Eisenhower, added two more divisions: there were to be two US beaches, *Utah* and *Omaha*, and three British–Canadian beaches, *Gold*, *Juno* and *Sword*. An elaborate deception plan, Operation *Fortitude*, persuaded the Germans that the invasion would be directed to the Pas de Calais by a notional 1st US Army Group based in Kent and Sussex. There was friction between Rundstedt, Commander-in-Chief West, and Rommel, whose army group held the invasion sector. The former favoured the classical solution to an invasion, hoping to defeat it once its main concentration was identified. The latter recognized that it would prove hard to concentrate armour in the face of Allied air superiority: he argued that tanks should be kept close to the beaches. Hitler's paranoid over-control did not help: Rundstedt quipped that the only soldiers he could move without permission were the sentries at his gates.

Bad weather forced Eisenhower to delay D-Day by 24 hours, but shortly after midnight on June 5, the first Allied airborne troops arrived in France, and by dawn two US airborne divisions – 82nd and 101st – and the British 6th had landed. The American divisions were widely spread, and some parachutists landed in rivers or inundations.

This helped keep the Germans guessing, and when the seaborne landings came after dawn there was no co-ordinated counterattack.

The landings themselves went well, except on "Bloody *Omaha*." Here a combination of bad luck and miscalculation combined in nightmarish landing. A combination of brave leadership, effective support from destroyers which came close inshore, and the fact that the defenders had neither adequate artillery ammunition nor a mobile reserve, helped the Americans get off the beach. But it had been a close run thing, with Lieutenant General Omar N. Bradley, commanding the US 1st Army, close to suspending further attacks, and cost the American some 2,000 casualties, as opposed to 200 on *Utah*.

By dusk on D-Day the Allies were securely ashore, though their beachheads had not yet linked up the British had failed to capture Caen. The Allies consolidated their position in the days that followed. Two prefabricated harbours – *Mulberries* – were built, at Arromanches in the British sector and around *Omaha* in the US sector. The American *Mulberry* was destroyed, and the British damaged, by an unseasonable gale but enough supplies were landed over open beaches to sustain the Allies. This was as well, for when the Americans took the port of Cherbourg on June 27, they found it systematically wrecked.

If the break-in to Normandy had gone well, the breakout proved harder. On the western flank the Americans struggled through the *bocage*, small fields bounded by hedged banks and linked by sunken lanes. On the eastern flank the British made heavy weather of capturing Caen. Montgomery maintained that he had always intended to attract German armour there to give the Americans a clear run in the west, and though the campaign showed less clarity than his postwar comments imply, this is generally what happened. On July 18, the British failed to advance as far in Operation *Goodwood* as the either the weight of preparatory bombing or the commitment of three armoured divisions suggests was their intention, but it did help to fix German armour.

Bradley mounted Operation *Cobra* just over a week later. Another heavy aerial bombardment softened up the German position, but the decision to commit armour against a crumbling defence was the decision of Lieutenant General "Lightning Joe" Collins, the corps commander on the spot. The Americans took

Avranches, and while some divisions curled down into Brittany, others swung eastwards. Bradley stepped up to command 12th Army Group, entrusting his own army to Courtney Hodges, and activating Patton's 3rd Army. Montgomery, still ground force commander, now disposed of Lieutenant General Harry Crerar's 1st Canadian Army and Dempsey's British 2nd in 21st Army Group, and Bradley's army group with 1st and 3rd US Armies. At Hitler's insistence Kluge, now Commander-in-Chief West, counterattacked at Mortain on August 7, making short-lived gains. Over the next two weeks the Germans were hemmed in between Montgomery in the north and Patton in the south as the Falaise pocket was formed. Although the Allies linked up on August 19, the neck of the pocket was not sealed for days, and key officers slipped through. But it was the end for most of the defenders of Normandy, and the killing fields below Mont Ormel bore testimony to the efficacy of air power against a compressed target.

Hitler, dismayed by news of landings on the French Riviera, granted permission to withdraw on August 16, and there was no prospect of defending either Paris or Brussels. The Allies seemed set fair to win the war that year: that they failed to do so says much for the recuperative powers of the German army, and the lack of clear strategy. Eisenhower was now land force as well as Supreme commander, and could not establish a rigid priority for a single thrust on a narrow front, especially when that thrust would have been in the Montgomery's sector. Operation *Market Garden*, a bold attempt to seize successive water obstacles in Holland and then push 30th Corps across them and on into Germany, narrowly failed despite the valour of the British 1st Airborne Division at Arnhem. Patton was bogged down on the Moselle, and further north Hodges fought hard for the Hurtgen Forest. Although the port of Antwerp was taken and its approaches cleared there was no decisive advance into Germany.

On December 16, the Germans launched an offensive in the Ardennes. Hitler hoped to retake Antwerp and, striking Allied armies at a point of junction, to fragment the alliance. Bad weather grounded Allied aircraft, and the Germans made good progress. Yet it could not last. When the skies cleared the Americans were not only able to drop supplies, but also to wreak havoc on German armour. By the year's end it was clear that Hitler's last gamble had failed.

THE BATTLE FOR MONTE CASSINO

In January 1944, the Allies attacked the Gustav Line, running across Italy south of Rome. Heavy fighting took place around Cassino, where the Rome–Naples road passes up the Liri Valley. There were four separate battles. In January, US troops were fought to a standstill at Cassino while the French Expeditionary Corps made progress in appalling terrain to the north. In February, New Zealand and Indian troops attacked Cassino and Monastery Hill. The third battle, a month later, saw further fighting for town and hill. In May a co-ordinated offensive, Operation *Diadem*, was successful and Polish troops occupied the monastery.

ABOVE

On February 15, the sixth-century Benedictine monastery, which looks down on Cassino, was heavily bombed. The decision to bomb remains deeply controversial: there were no Germans in it when it was attacked, though its ruins made excellent defences.

RIGHT

Cassino itself was heavily bombed on March 15, at the start of the third battle. Men of the 2nd New Zealand Division attacked the town itself, while the 4th Indian Division attacked the heights above. Castle Hill (top right), the scene of fierce fighting, was taken.

LEFT

First aid men dash through the ruins of Cassino to help the wounded, March 16. Although the fighting was vicious, the Red Cross was generally honoured, and on at least one occasion British stretchers were borrowed – and returned – by the Germans.

BELOW

Men of General Wladyslaw Anders' 2nd Polish Corps using grenades in the mountains above Cassino, May 1944. Anders' men had been captured by the Russians in 1939, travelled to the Middle East via Iran in 1942, and fought with distinction in Italy.

ABOVE

A British 6-pdr anti-tank gun in the
ruins of Sant'Angelo in the valley below
Cassino. The village had been the scene
of a disastrous river crossing by the
US 36th Infantry Division in January,
and was taken, after heavy fighting,
during Operation *Diadem*.

ABOVE

View of Cassino after heavy
bombardment showing a knocked-out
Sherman tank by a Bailey bridge in
the foreground with Monastery Ridge
and Castle Hill in the background.

LEFT
German prisoners of war
after the battle of Monte Cassino.

RIGHT
A British soldier with a Bren gun
in the ruins of Cassino, May 18, 1944.

LEFT
French women and children, who
were unable to return home after
the outbreak of war, lay flowers on
the grave of an unknown British soldier,
May 19, 1944. They did this every day.

THE GERMAN RETREAT IN ITALY

In late 1943, the Allies planned a landing south of Rome. The project was scrapped but then revived as Operation *Shingle*, and 6th US Corps, commanded by Major General John Lucas of the 5th Army landed at Anzio and Nettuno on January 22. The plan was not well conceived. The landing did not provoke German withdrawal from the Gustav Line, and although Lucas might have entered Rome in a rapid advance, he lacked the strength to hold it. After severe fighting around the Anzio beachead, the allies broke out in late May as Operation *Diadem* forced the Gustav Line.

ABOVE

This shot, from the collection of the Luftwaffe commander Field Marshal Wolfram von Richthofen (right) shows Field Marshal Albert Kesselring, the very capable German Commander in Chief at a forward command post in the Nettuno sector.

ABOVE
The Anzio landings began well.
Here German prisoners watch
landing craft unloading.

LEFT
Men of a heavy anti-aircraft battery digging
in, March 1944. Flak guns were manned by
the Luftwaffe: the soldier on the right wears
the distinctive Luftwaffe eagle on his helmet.

Captured German paratroopers
carry a British soldier who has lost
a foot to a mine, May 1944.

BELOW
US Rangers made a disastrous attempt
to capture Cisterna on January 30,
losing over 700 men. This is the
town on May 25, after its capture.

ABOVE
Another Italian river: British troops crossing the Melfa, May 1944.

RIGHT
A flak gun defends the Eternal City: Rome, June 1944.

ABOVE
Lieutenant General Mark Clark of
5th Army regarded Rome as the real
prize of the campaign, and duly took
it on June 4. A delighted Roosevelt
commented: "The first Axis capital
is in our hands. One up and two to go."

LEFT
Pisa, with its famous leaning tower,
fell in July, but another strong position,
the Gothic Line lay just to the north.

ABOVE
There was an active Italian resistance,
in which the communists played a
leading role: some 40,000 of its
members died. Here a German light
flak gun takes on partisans, winter 1943–44.

BURMA

In Burma the tide of war turned later than in other theatres, and much depended on the level-headed General Sir William Slim, commander of the 14th Army. In February 1943, Brigadier Orde Wingate's Chindits raided deep behind Japanese lines, doing much for battered British morale. In 1944 the Allies planned a three-pronged offensive, in the coastal Arakan; with the second and much larger Chindit operation; and with Chinese–American forces in the north-east. However, the Japanese mounted a pre-emptive attack that to fierce fighting in the Arakan and at Imphal and Kohima. The Japanese army fell back in July after the most serious defeat in its history, Slim followed it, crossing the Chindwin in December.

BELOW

Originally captioned as "Troops surveying the destruction in a Burma village," this photograph in fact shows Brigadier "Mad Mike" Calvert (left), a column commander in the first Chindit expedition and a brigade commander in the second, with Lieutenant Colonel Shaw and (right) Major James Rutherford Lumley, father of the actress Joanna Lumley.

ABOVE

Allied airpower played a crucial role in Burma. Here Hurri-bombers attack a bridge on the Tiddim road.

BELOW
Chindits crossing a river. Bernard
Fergusson, a column commander in the
first expedition, wrote that only 95 of
his 318 men survived. More than 30
had to be abandoned on a sand-bank during
the night crossing of a fast-flowing river.

OPPOSITE PAGE
A Cecil Beaton photograph of a Gurkha
carrying a wounded comrade during the
fighting in the Arakan, January 1944.

ABOVE
Troops scrambling up
an Arakan hillside, early 1944.

RIGHT
Tanks were useful for the close-range
reduction of Japanese strongpoints:
this Grant helps clear the Ngakydauk
Pass in the Arakan. It was passed
by the censor in May 1944.

Sikhs of the 7th Indian
Division in the Ngakydauk Pass area.

A Hurricane being prepared for another
ground attack sortie, Arakan 1944.

The little town of Kohima, 4,000
feet up in the Naga Hills, commanded
the main supply route to beleaguered
Imphal and was the subject of fierce, but
unavailing Japanese attacks in April and
May. This photograph shows the Naga
village, part of the Kohima battlefield.

RIGHT

Galahad, a US volunteer force often known as Merrill's Marauders, captured Myitkyina in Northern Burma in August. These men of the *Mars* task force, including some of the now disbanded Marauders, then advanced from Myitkynia towards Mandalay.

LEFT

Lieutenant General Joseph Stilwell, Commander in Chief of US and Chinese forces in the China–India–Burma theatre, with Brigadier General Frank D. Merrill. Stilwell's cantankerous personality earned him the nickname "Vinegar Joe", but his capture of Myitktkina opened up a shorter air supply route into China than the dangerous trip over the "Hump".

OPPOSITE PAGE TOP

No less than ninety-six per cent of supplies to the 14th Army in Burma went by air. Here a bullock is loaded into a C-47 transport aircraft.

OPPOSITE PAGE BOTTOM

Although Indian troops had the lion's share of the fighting in Burma, Africans also played an important part. This photograph shows men of the 11th East African Division near Kalewa on the Chindwin during Slim's advance, December 1944.

LEFT
LEFT
The first phase of Operation *Bagration*, began on June 23, and ripped the heart out of Army Group Centre. In its second phase the Russians exploited their advantage: here T-34s strike deep into Lithuania in July.

RUSSIA ADVANCES

In 1944 the Red Army continued to its inexorable movement westwards, taking Odessa in April and Sevastapol in May, and destroying Army Group Centre in the great Byeorussian offensive of June–July. Romania surrendered in August, Finland made terms in September and Bulgaria changed sides the same month. By the end of the year, the Russians had captured Belgrade, encircled Budapest, and were braced for the final offensive which would take them deep into Germany.

RIGHT
The Russians encircled Budapest by December 26. Pest fell in mid-January, 1945, but it took the Russians another month to take Buda. This tank has crashed through a sewer in a Budapest street.

SCĂ PARTIDUL COMUNIST
DIN ROMANIA

ABOVE
On August 23, King Michael of Romania had Marshal Antonescu, who had been reluctant to abandon his German allies, arrested: Romania signed an Armistice on September 12. The Russians quickly consolidated their position and installed a puppet government in March 1945. These Romanian communists acclaim the armistice.

RIGHT
The Finns signed the armistice with Russia on September 19, buying freedom from Soviet occupation with a heavy price in territory. This photograph shows the Finnish peace delegation arriving at the frontier before flying to Moscow.

WARSAW UPRISING

In mid-1942 the Germans began deportations from the Warsaw
Ghetto to extermination camps, but when they moved in to liquidate
the ghetto in 1943, there was unexpectedly fierce resistance.
On August 1, 1944, there was a more serious rising by over
37,000 Home Army fighters under Lieutenant General Tadeusz
Bor-Komorowski, which lasted until he surrendered on terms in
October. The Russians were close to Warsaw but did little to
help, inducing many historians to suggest that it was in
Stalin's interests to let Warsaw's resistance elite be crushed.

ABOVE
So near but so far: a Russian machine-gunner
on the banks of the Vistula, August 10, 1944.

BELOW
German civilians captured by the Home Army
were made to wear this distinctive dress.

At the beginning of the Warsaw Uprising few members of the Home Army were properly armed, but weapons and equipment were captured from the Germans or received from Soviet or Western supply drops.

A wounded member of the Home Army emerges from a sewer after the Polish surrender.

RIGHT

The surrender unusually granted Polish combatants the right to be regarded as such: defiant women fighters march into captivity.

BELOW

This carefully orchestrated German photograph shows Bor-Komorowski surrendering to a smiling SS Obergruppenführer Erich von dem Bach-Zelewski, commander of the German counterattack force. Polish killed, civilian and military, may have exceeded 250,000, and much of Warsaw was destroyed.

THE PACIFIC WAR

In 1944 MacArthur and Halsey pushed across the Pacific, their main thrusts converging towards the Philippines. The costly capture of Tarawa in November 1943, provided evidence that helped future operations. Vice Admiral Spruance took the Marshall Islands in January and February, and then, in June, attacked the Marianas, bringing about the naval battle of the Philippine Sea. MacArthur's forces, meanwhile, had completed their conquest of New Guinea. That autumn the Joint Chiefs redefined strategy for the Pacific theatre. MacArthur and Halsey would first converge on Leyte. MacArthur would then invade Luzon, while Halsey struck at Iwo Jima and Okinawa.

The island of Saipan in the Marianas housed a powerful Japanese garrison. US Marines landed on June 15, and the island was taken on July 9, after vicious fighting. Here attackers use grenades as they fight their way through a Japanese position.

ABOVE

A US Navy corpsman administers blood
plasma to a wounded Marine, one of
over 15,000 US casualties on Saipan.
Blood transfusion, in its infancy in the
First World War, made a major contribution
to improved survival rates: some
four-and-a-half percent of wounded
American soldiers died, down from
eight percent in the First World War.

LEFT

A Japanese aircraft crashes into the sea during the Battle of the Philippine Sea, June 19–20. Nicknamed by the Americans "The Great Marianas Turkey Shoot", this huge carrier battle of the war saw better-trained US pilots, aided by excellent intelligence, destroy over 300 Japanese aircraft for the loss of about 130, many of whose crews were saved.

BELOW

A US heavy cruiser bombards the island of Guam, largest of the Marianas, from close range before landing on July 20. The Japanese lost over 10,000, over ten times US losses: the last Japanese soldier surrendered in 1972.

ABOVE
US paratroops drop on to Noemfoor
Island in the Dutch East Indies, July 4.

US landing craft run in for the landings on the Philippine island of Leyte, October 20.

RIGHT

The Japanese conceived an ambitious plan to lure Halsey's 3rd Fleet northwards while they crushed the Leyte landings and the smaller US 7th Fleet protecting them. The result was the biggest naval battle ever fought, which ended in Japanese defeat. Here the massive 72,800 ton battleship *Musashi* is under attack on October 24: she turned turtle and sank after receiving multiple bomb and torpedo hits.

ABOVE

The acme of propaganda shots shows
MacArthur wading ashore on Leyte in
October, thus making good his 1942
promise to return to the Philippines.

THE NORMANDY LANDINGS

D-Day, the Allied invasion of France on June 6, 1944, was the largest amphibious operation in history. Planning began in 1943, and it was quickly decided that the Bay of the Seine offered better prospects than the closer but more obvious Pas de Calais or more distant Brittany. Three airborne divisions (two US, one British) secured the flanks of the landings on five beaches, *Utah* and *Omaha* for the Americans and *Gold*, *Juno* and *Sword* for the British and Canadians.

ABOVE
US Paratroops have a last-minute equipment check before boarding their Dakota aircraft in southern England.

RIGHT
The landing zone of the 6th British Airborne Division near the Normandy village of Ranville. Paratroops were, of necessity, lightly equipped: heavier weapons were flown in by gliders, many of which can be seen here.

BELOW
Infantry of the US 7th Corps move
over the sea wall on *Utah* beach at the
western end of the Allied landings.

One of the many Robert Capa photographs which helped inspire the early sequences in the movie *Saving Private Ryan*, shows men of Company E, 116th Regimental Combat Team among obstacles on the shoreline of "Bloody *Omaha*". The Germans held the sandy cliffs just inland; their positions had not been badly damaged by naval or air bombardment and most of the amphibious tanks meant to accompany the assaulting infantry sank in the choppy sea.

Infantry of the 3rd Canadian Division's Régiment de la Chaudière land on *Juno* Beach. The Anglo–Canadian landings emphasized the importance of getting tanks and specialist beach-clearing vehicles ashore before the bulk if the infantry.

ABOVE

A scene on *Queen White* sector of *Sword* Beach. Men of the 1st Battalion The South Lancashire regiment in 3rd Division's first assault wave, with amphibious tanks of A Squadron, 13th/18th Hussars in the background.

RIGHT

The Allies knew that the Germans would defend and then destroy French ports. The components of two prefabricated *Mulberry* harbours were towed to France after D-Day. Although the US harbour off *Omaha* beach was badly damaged by a storm on June 19, the British *Mulberry* off Arromanches, shown here, survived.

ABOVE

The Normandy Landings were a
logistic operation of unprecedented
scale. Here American landing ships unload
while engineers work on clearing beach
obstacles and preparing routes inland.

ALLIED ADVANCE AND LIBERATION

D-Day was only the beginning. After it the Allies faced a long and difficult battle to break out of Normandy, and some of the fighting in the Summer of 1944 resembled the attritional battles of the First World War. The Americans eventually broke out on the western flank in late July, and the Allies, now forming the British–Canadian 21st Army Group under General Montgomery and US 12th Army Group under Bradley, encircled much of the German army in the Falaise Pocket. Thereafter the advance was swift, and by the end of August it seemed that victory was in sight.

BELOW

The sharp end of war. A section of British infantry, its men with bayonets fixed and an abundance of ammunition, led by its corporal with a sten-gun, advance on June 26, during Operation *Epsom*, an unsuccessful attempt to outflank the key city of Caen from the west.

ABOVE

Although the censor has obscured his unit-title this Bren-gunner's divisional flash (a double "T" for Tyne-Tees) identifies him as a member of the 50th (Northumbrian) Division, which went ashore on *Gold* Beach and fought in the Bayeux area. The Bren was accurate and robust, but lacked the firepower of German belt-fed machine guns.

German units moving up to Normandy were harassed by Allied air attacks and Resistance sabotage. On June 10, a unit of 2nd SS Panzer Division massacred 642 civilians in the village of Oradour-sur Glane near Limoges. No clear motive has been established, but revenge for the abduction of a German officer has been suggested.

Men of the 2nd Battalion The Royal Warwickshire Regiment advance through a wheatfield during Operation *Charnwood*, which took Caen on July 7–9 in the wake of the bombing raid which did terrible damage to the city.

RIGHT
There was sometimes light relief even in Normandy. The original caption notes that Derby Day (June 18) "was observed by British troops – even though on a small scale because of more urgent duties." Sergeant A.A. Dalziel, Royal Signals, is the amateur bookmaker and Lance Corporal Day (demonstrating how his wool cap-comforter should not be worn) acts as his clerk.

ABOVE
In August the Canadians fought their way down the Caen-Falaise road in Operations *Totalize* and *Tractable*. A Canadian column passes the village of Rocquancourt, to the west of the road, where smoke rises from fires caused by bombing and shelling.

ABOVE

The western flank of Normandy was characterized by small fields separated by hedged banks in a countryside called bocage. "I didn't want to stand up and slug …" remarked Bradley, "but … while in this bocage … we could do nothing else." The shot was taken on July 31, after the *Cobra* breakout.

The French Resistance initially comprised heterogeneous groups which often pursued diverse aims by different methods. From February 1944, the Resistance, at least in theory, was brought together as the *Forces Françaises de l'Intérieur*. This jubilant FFI man, with a British-supplied Bren gun, is in the recently liberated town of Châteaudun.

BELOW

Collaborators were mistreated or killed. On Bastille Day, July 14, these Cherbourg women, accused of sexual collaboration, had their hair shorn and were paraded around the town. The anguished mother of one such victim observed that her daughter would have slept with Americans too: it was her job.

ABOVE

A US medic gives roadside first aid
to a German officer, shot up in
his staff car, Chartres, August 17.

LEFT

In Paris the Resistance rose as the liberators
– French men of General Leclerc's 2nd
Armoured Division – approached. Tanks
in action in front of Notre Dame de Paris.

OPPOSITE PAGE

A powerful icon: Americans
stop their jeep to admire the Eiffel Tower.

ABOVE
German prisoners are marched down
the Rue de Rivoli in Paris under FFI guard.

ABOVE

De Gaulle triumphant. On August 26,
he walked down the Champs Elysées
to huge popular acclaim and went on
to Notre Dame were he stood
unmoved when firing broke out.

SOUTHERN FRANCE

The French Riviera Landings (Operation *Anvil/Dragoon*) took place on August 15, after much Anglo–American debate. Initially conceived to distract German attention from Normandy, they were not popular with the British, who favoured concentration in Western France or a thrust from Italy into Austria. US General Alexander Patch's 7th Army comprised British and French elements and made good progress once through the crust of beach defence. The operation proved useful, as southern French ports handled a third of the 1.3 million tons of supplies that reached US forces in October.

RIGHT
Landing craft move supplies ashore in Southern France.

BELOW
Air interdiction: American B-26 Marauder bombers scoring a direct hit on the railway bridge over the Rhône at Arles.

MARKET GARDEN

Operation *Market Garden* was a bold plan designed to use the three divisions of the 1st Allied Airborne Army to take bridges over the water obstacles in front of Montogomery, and to exploit with a thrust into the German heartland. Landings by the US 82nd and 101st Airborne Divisions secured the southern crossings, but although 1st British Airborne Division took the northern end of Arnhem Bridge, ground forces took too long to reach it and the bulk of the parachutists were killed or captured.

ABOVE
Men of the 1st Airborne Division on their way to Arnhem, September 17.

RIGHT
Parachutists land among gliders at Wolfheze, west of Arnhem. This main dropping zone was too far from British objectives: it took four hours for paratroops to reach them on foot, by which time the German defence was hardening.

LEFT

Paratroops heading for Arnhem are given welcome refreshment by the Dutch on September 17. The helmeted figure looking at the camera is Private W.M Hill of the mortar platoon, 3rd Parachute Battalion, carrying part of the 3-inch mortar and two of its bombs in his jump bag.

BELOW

Elements of two SS panzer divisions were refitting near Arnhem, but warnings of their presence had been ignored. These men of the 4th Polizei-Panzergrenadierdivision await fresh parachute landings.

LEFT

Most of the 1st Airborne Division was pushed into a perimeter at Oosterbeek, where this soldier, armed with a US M-1 carbine, defends a house.

BELOW

Paratroops of the US 82nd Airborne Division unload a wrecked glider near Nijmegen. The American drops succeeded, but the British assault proved, as Lieutenant General Browning had suspected to be a "bridge too far".

THE BATTLE OF THE BULGE

In December Hitler launched a desperate counteroffensive in the
snowy hills of the Ardennes, hoping to cause a crisis in the Allied
command and capture Antwerp. 6th SS Panzer Army attacked
alongside 5th Panzer Army, with 7th Army covering their southern
flank. Bad weather and lack of preparation by the US contributed to
their initial success, but 101st Airborne Division held near Bastogne.
When the weather cleared Allied aircraft wreaked havoc and Patton
hooked into the Bulge from the south. Allied commanders were
indeed ruffled but the blow lacked sufficient weight to do long-term
damage, and Germany could not replace men and tanks lost.

ABOVE
German troops dash past a
burning American vehicle on
the attack's first day, December 16.

BELOW
1st SS Panzer Division advanced in parallel battle groups, its most aggressive led by SS Lieutenant Colonel Jochen Peiper. Although usually identified as Peiper, this is in fact not him. A signpost points to Malmédy, where 84 US soldiers were murdered, for which Peiper was condemned to death, a sentence later commuted.

A recently caught young SS man is brought in by a patrol of 82nd Airborne on the northern edge of the bulge.

LEFT
C-47s drop much needed medical supplies and ammunition to the encircled 101st Airborne Division in Bastogne, Christmas Day.

OPPOSITE
Some English-speaking Germans dressed in American uniforms, helped create confusion behind the Allied lines. Those captured were shot by firing squad: here military policemen tie a resolute Günther Billing to the execution stake.

VI AND V2S

B-weapons were the British name for the *Vergeltungswaffen* (retaliation weapons) developed by the Germans. The V-1 flying bomb was a small pilotless jet aircraft, about 10,000 of which were launched against England. The V-2 was a ballistic rocket: some 500 were fired at Antwerp and more than 1,000 at England. These weapons came as a rude shock to the population of London and the Home Counties, which had came to believe that German air attacks were now a thing of the past.

ABOVE
V-1s could be shot down or, as we see here, flipped to destruction by a Spitfire, which flew alongside and flipped the flying bomb's wing on its own.

RIGHT
A V-2 undergoing final refuelling and adjustment of its controls. The weapons could be launched from small, easily concealed sites.

ABOVE

The result of a V-2 attack. Police Constable
Frederick Godwin, stationed at Gipsy Hill in
South London, consoling a man who had
gone to walk the dog while his wife cooked
Sunday lunch. He returned to find his street
demolished and his wife buried beneath the
ruins. PC Godwin's daughter wrote to the
Imperial War Museum to identify him
adding: "My father was a good and caring
man, and these photos personify that for us."

FOLLOWING PAGE

A female Air Raid Warden comforts a child
rescued from a house destroyed by a V-1, June 23.

LEFT
Workers in Leningrad putting finishing touches to a gun. In 1944 alone, Russian factories turned out 129,500 guns and mortars and almost 30,000 tanks.

BELOW
Dr Joseph Goebbels, the German propaganda minister, toured bombed cities, and in 1944 became Reich Plenipotentiary for Total War, introducing a 60-hour week.

HOME FRONTS

The Second World War blurred distinctions between combatants and non-combatants. Civilians not only toiled to produce war material, but in many theatres ran the risk of air attack or ground invasion. Although women had always been involved in wars, conflict on this scale both increased the participation of women and made it more visible. Women made a contribution that demands acknowledgement. Nonna Alexandrovna Smirnova, a Russian anti-aircraft gunner was, perhaps, not overstating the case when she wrote, long after the war:

> "You must tell your children,
> Putting modesty aside,
> That without us, without women,
> There would have been no spring in 1945."

LEFT
Liberty ships were mass-produced merchantmen made in US yards. Over 2,700 were constructed, one in less than five days. These two Liberty ships await final fitting out in an east-coast shipyard.

BELOW
WAAFs at an RAF glider station repairing parachutes, May 31, 1944.

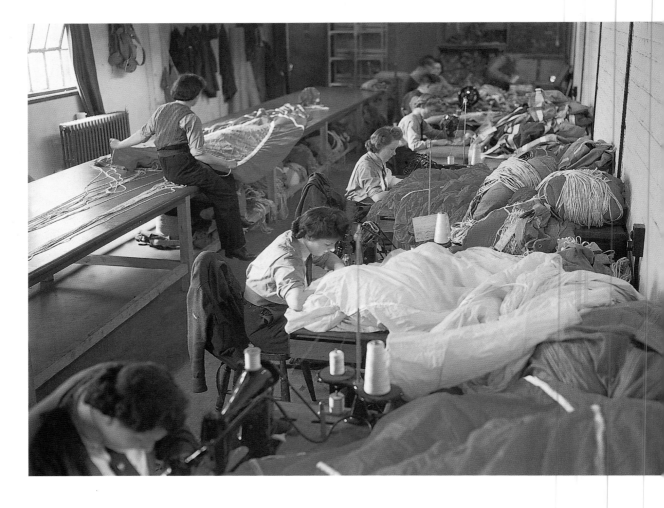

LEFT
"Bevin Boy" Jim Walters, working in a Kent colliery. The "Bevin Boy" scheme, named after Ernest Bevin, British Minister of Labour, was introduced in 1943. One young conscript in every ten was chosen by ballot to serve in the mines rather than in the armed forces.

RIGHT
Perhaps a little less glamorous than the "Rosie the Riveter" featured in posters, this woman war worker is tapering .50 caliber cartridges at Frankford Arsenal, Philadelphia.

LEFT

On July 20, 1944, a bomb planted in Hitler's conference room narrowly failed to kill him: here he shows Mussolini the damage. Although there was no mass resistance movement in Germany, many Germans did work for the overthrow of Hitler, at the risk, and often the cost, of their lives and those of their families: the bomb plot was the pretext for almost 5,000 executions.

BELOW

Over 7,000 of the Avro Lancaster 1 heavy bombers were built, each with four Rolls Royce Merlin engines. And this was by no means the most numerous British bomber; there were over 11,000 Wellingtons and nearly 8,000 Mosquitos.

ABOVE
Carrying old Moisin-Nagant rifles, whose bayonets were permanently fixed in the belief that this encouraged aggression, these women are part of a Russian partisan group. Between 500,000 and a million Russians fought with the partisans.

RIGHT
As American air power made its weight felt, Japan experienced air raids, made particularly destructive by the flammable materials used in the construction of many houses. These Tokyo students are preparing an air raid shelter.

1 9 4 5
TO THE BITTER END

AS 1945 BEGAN GERMANY'S PLIGHT WAS HOPELESS, BUT NEITHER HITLER'S APOCALYPTIC VISION NOR ALLIED INSISTENCE ON UNCONDITIONAL SURRENDER OFFERED ANY PROSPECT OF A COMPROMISE PEACE, AND THE WAR AGAINST GERMANY WAS FOUGHT TO A BITTER END THAT SAW MOST GERMAN TOWNS REDUCED TO RUBBLE AND BERLIN TAKEN BY ASSAULT.

IN THE PACIFIC the Americans gradually strengthened their grip on Japan, taking Iwo Jima and Okinawa, and putting themselves in position to mount a direct assault on the Japanese home islands. Even in Burma there was now no stopping the Allies, who swept down to take Mandalay and Rangoon. On August 6 and 9 atomic bombs were dropped on the Japanese cities of Hiroshima and Nagasaki, bringing swift acceptance of peace terms, and a surrender ceremony aboard USS *Missouri* in Tokyo Bay formally brought the war to an end.

In 1945 the Red Army advanced on Berlin in two gigantic strides. On January 12, it began an assault which took it from the Vistula to the Oder, so close to Berlin that Russian troops could see the nightly glow of the fires caused by Allied bombing. A piece of bold opportunism enabled the Russians to seize a bridgehead over the Oder near Kustrin, and they resisted all German attempts to push them back. In January Hitler unwisely made Heinrich Himmler, head of the SS, commander of Army Group Vistula, blocking the direct Russian approach to Berlin, but the appointment was such a disaster that Himmler was succeeded by the level-headed Colonel General Gotthard Heinrici. Heinrici, all too well aware of the ferocious artillery bombardment that would preceded the Russian attack on his position on the Seelow heights, west of the Oder, laid out a series of defensive lines, planning to vacate the first, in the low-lying Oderbruch, just before the bombardment began.

The Russians planned to used two fronts – army groups – for the drive on Berlin. Marshal Zhukov's 1st Byelorussian Front was to attack across the Seelow heights while Marshal Ivan Koniev's 1st Ukrainian Front swung in from the south. Stalin, who knew of the

rivalry between the two marshals, left the details of the final assault vague, implying that the city centre could be taken by whoever reached it first. The offensive began on April 16: Vienna had fallen three days before, and the Reich was rocking under the weight of blows from all directions. Zhukov, however, made heavy weather of Heinrici's defence, piling in his tank armies before his combined arms armies had cleared the Oderbruch and prodigally expending men and tanks. It was bludgeon against rapier, and the Germans simply could not hold. Koniev's men made better progress, reaching Jüterbog, south of the capital, on April 20, while Zhukov closed on the Berlin outer defence ring the following day: on the April 25, the two fronts linked near Potsdam, completing Berlin's encirclement. Hitler, in his bunker under the Reich Chancellory, continued to spin fantastic schemes for the city's relief, and as Russian troops assaulted the Reichstag on April 30, he killed himself, having nominated Grand Admiral Karl Dönitz as his successor. Lieutenant General Karl Weidling surrendered the city on May 2.

Stalin's urgency was fuelled by the advance of the Western Allies. Early in the year they set about clearing the approaches to the Rhine, which Eisenhower had decided to cross on a broad front. There was hard fighting in bad weather, with the Anglo–Canadian battle for the Reichswald forest south-west of Cleves taking on characteristics all too redolent of parts of the Western Front in the First World War. Hodges's men bounced a crossing over the bridge at Remagen on March 7, and, although the sector was in unsuitable for a major breakout Hitler was furious, and replaced Rundstedt (yet again Commander-in-Chief West) with Kesselring. On March 22–23 Patton crossed the Rhine at Oppenheim, south of Mainz, and the following night Montgomery began his own characteristically deliberate crossing at Emmerich, Rees and Wesel. There were further crossings in the days that followed, and by early April the last natural obstacle between the western Allies and the German heartland was comprehensively breached.

The end was now so evidently in sight that German forces began to disintegrate, although harsh discipline was used to shore up flagging morale as flying courts-martial imposed summary death-sentences on genuine deserters as well as those unlucky enough to be found away from their units without verifiable cause. And parts of the Wehrmacht fought, remorselessly, to the end, although resistance to the Anglo–Americans tended to be less desperate than that against the Russians.

In late March the US 1st and 9th Armies enveloped the Ruhr, meeting near Paderborn on April 1 and encircling the bulk of Army Group B, whose commander, Field Marshal Walter Model – a thorough professional whose tendency to be called in in crises had earned him the nickname "the Führer's fireman" – duly shot himself. Patton took Frankfurt on March 29, and on April 12, 9th Army reached the Elbe near Magdeburg. On April 25, Russians and Americans met near Torgau, and the British met the Russians on the Baltic on May 2. There were several surrender ceremonies. On May 4, on Lüneberg Heath Montgomery accepted the surrender of Dönitz's plenipotentiaries. Three days later there was a more formal ceremony at Rheims, and the Russians ensured that the process was repeated at Karlshorst, on the edge of Berlin.

The war in Italy had ended slightly earlier. Colonel General Heinrich von Vietinghoff inherited an impossible task from Kesselring in early March, and as the weather improved Allied air power ravaged his lines of communications. 8th Army began its attack on April 9, and 5th Army's was launched on the April 14, catching the Germans off balance and taking Bologna. It was typical of the German plight that the redoubtable Senger, defender of Cassino, had to abandon his car before crossing the Po and then march 25 kilometres on its north bank. Benito Mussolini had been rescued from captivity on the Gran Sasso by a daring raid by SS Captain Otto Skorzeny in September 1943 and installed as head of a German puppet state, the Italian Social Republic. In late April 1945 he concluded that the game was up, and set off for Switzerland with his mistress, a handful of adherents, and a fortune in gold. He was caught by the partisans near Lake Como on the night of April 28, and promptly shot. Mussolini's erstwhile allies surrendered at Caserta on May 2.

There had never been much real strategic linkage between Germany and Japan, although the need to fight both adversaries stretched even the resources of the United States. The defeat of Germany made Japan's strategic position infinitely worse, for it would permit the western Allies to concentrate on a single enemy, and, although the Japanese could do no more than guess at it, Stalin had undertaken to attack Japan three months after the ending of the German war, and was to prove as good as his word, declaring war on August 8, and moving into Manchuria the next day. In November 1944 B-29 bombers based in the Marianas had begun bombing Japan, and the tiny volcanic island of Iwo Jima, half way between the Marianas and Japan, was required as an emergency airfield. The Americans landed on February 19, but the island was not secured until March 26, and the – posed – photograph of the raising of the American flag on Mount Suribachi, the extinct volcano that dominates the island, was symbolic of another hard-won victory.

The much larger island of Okinawa was invaded by Lieutenant General Simon Bolivar Buckner's 10th Army on April 1, after five days of fierce bombardment. The initial landings went deceptively well, but when the invaders were inland the defenders hit back with their customary determination. An attempt to support the garrison with a powerful naval squadron failed with the loss of the battleship *Yamato*, but the Japanese stepped up attacks by kamikaze suicide aircraft on the invasion fleet, sinking 21 ships and damaging another 66, 43 of them so badly that they had to be scrapped. General Buckner was killed by shellfire on June 18, but four days later his opponent, Lieutenant General Ushijima Mitsuru committed suicide after a defence which had cost the lives of all but 7,400 of his 77,000 troops and 20,000 local militia. The Americans quickly built 22 airstrips on Okinawa, and soon 18 air groups of bombers and their fighter escorts were operating from the island.

In Burma, meanwhile, 14th Army's offensive gained momentum following its crossing of the Chindwin in December 1944. In February and March 1945 Slim fought the brilliantly staged battle of Mandalay–Meiktila, first feinting towards Mandalay and then hooking round the Japanese flank and across the Irrawaddy to take the communication centre of Meiktila. The new commander of Burma Area Army (his predecessor had been dismissed after Imphal–Kohima), Lieutenant General Kimura Hyotaro, counterattacked quickly, but was unable to shake Slim's grip. Mandalay itself was taken after fierce fighting of great symbolic importance, for it was said that "who rules Mandalay rules Burma." Slim paused briefly at Pyawbwe, but the road to Rangoon lay open, and his men hustled on down it. It was the apotheosis of the old British Indian army, men of twenty races, a dozen religions and a score of languages, surely never more effective at any time in its long history. The Burmese capital duly fell to an amphibious attack, Operation *Dracula*, on May 3.

The capture of Okinawa had cost the Americans 7,613 killed and 31,807 wounded, and emphasized just how costly an assault on the Japanese home islands was likely to be. This was at least part of the reason why President Harry S. Truman, who succeeded Roosevelt when the latter died suddenly on April 12, used the first atomic weapons against Japan, and while members of postwar generations harbour doubts about the morality of this action, there were far fewer concerns at the time, not least amongst the soldiers, sailors and airmen who would have risked their lives in the assault on Japan. But it is also clear that using the bomb against the Japanese was designed to demonstrate its effectiveness to the Russians. The Allied conference at Yalta in February 1945 had focused on the organization of the postwar world, and it was one of the conflict's many ironies that the Poles who had fought so gallantly in Italy, France, Poland and Germany were to find that the postwar borders of their country were to be moved westwards, leaving the eastern part of Poland in Russian hands while gains to the west were made at German expense: the new frontier was to run along the rivers Oder and Neisse. In July and August the last wartime conference was held in Potsdam, and it was there that Truman told Stalin of the atomic bomb's existence.

By 1920 it was believed that a supremely powerful weapon might be created by the fission of heavy nuclei or the fusion of light ones, and by 1940 German Jewish physicists working in England suggested that a tiny amount of Uranium 235 could form the basis for a powerful bomb. British-based scientists were shifted to the American research team, the "Manhattan Project", in 1942, and the first nuclear explosion, *Trinity*, took place at Alamagordo in New Mexico on 16 July 1945. News of the project's success induced Truman, as Churchill put it, to stand up to the Russians "in a most emphatic and decisive manner." Two bombs were dropped on Hiroshima and Nagasaki in early August, and assurances that the doctrine of unconditional surrender would be modified so as to enable the emperor to remain on his throne induced the Japanese to surrender on August 14. The use of atomic weapons not only helped end the war, but cast a long and enduring shadow over the postwar world. The alliance that had won the war broke down, all too swiftly, as the iron curtain described by Churchill in 1946 descended across a scarred Europe.

One of the most striking effects of the postwar division of the world into two rival power-blocs was to make balanced appreciation of the Second World War almost impossible, as Anglo–American historians generally failed to do full justice to Russian achievements in the east, while the Russians, for their part, did not acknowledge the importance of the Anglo–American contribution. As we enter the Twenty-First Century at least that imbalance is corrected, and the Second World War stands clearly for what it was: the most momentous event in the whole of human history, in which a great alliance (with its own huge flaws, contradictions and inconsistencies) brought down a regime of unprecedented vileness. It is a tragedy that, like their fathers before them who had endured another great war, the war's combatants, and the civilians who supported them, did not quite get the world to which they were entitled: yet this should overshadow neither their endeavour nor their sacrifice.

SOVIET ADVANCE INTO GERMANY

On January 12, the Red Army began the Vistula–Oder operation, and by February 3, it was on the Oder, within striking distance of Berlin. While the Russians paused, consolidating in East and West Prussia, Hitler launched the 6th SS Panzer Army, redeployed from the west, in a vain offensive in Hungary. The Russians grabbed a bridgehead over the Oder in February, and on April 16, they began the Berlin operation, with Zhukov's 1st Byelorussian Front vying with Koniev's 1st Ukrainian Front for the honour of capturing the capital. After a destructive battle Berlin surrendered on May 2.

ABOVE
Hitler used the very old and the very young to defend the Reich: these prisoners were taken in Silesia in February.

RIGHT
Königsberg, capital of East Prussia, was taken by the Russians in early April. It became the Russian city of Kaliningrad when national boundaries were realigned after the war.

LEFT
A column of Russian tanks rolls down a Berlin street.

BELOW
In one of the war's classic photographs the Russian flag is raised over the Reichstag in Berlin, May 2. Some of the shots in the sequence needed subtle retouching to conceal the fact that the flag-raising sergeant had an armful of "liberated" watches.

DISCOVERY OF THE CONCENTRATION CAMPS

As the Allies advanced they found horrifying evidence of the fate of the Jews, gypsies, homosexuals and enemies of the Nazi regime. Death camps like Auschwitz-Birkenau were partially destroyed before the Allied troops reached them, but concentration camps such as Bergen-Belsen and Dachau were horrifying enough. It is impossible to be sure of the real toll of those killed in death camps, concentration camps, ghettos, labour camps or forced marches, but it included some six million European Jews and at least 3½ million Soviet prisoners of war.

RIGHT
Crematoria in the camp at Lublin-Majdanek, reached the Red Army in July 1944.

BELOW
A communal grave at Bergen-Belsen, a concentration camp liberated by the British in April 1945. It then contained 10,000 unburied dead and mass graves with 40,000 bodies. Many of the 60,000 survivors died soon after liberation.

RIGHT
Survivors of the concentration camp
at Dachau celebrate their release
by the US 45th Infantry Division.

BELOW

The camp at Buchenwald was liberated
by the Americans on April 13. Citizens
form the nearby town of Weimar
were marched round the camp by
American military policemen to ensure
that its sights were not forgotten.

ITALY

Filthy weather, a stout defence and the diversion of troops to Southern France prevented the Allies form completing the conquest of Italy in 1944. The Allies began their main attack in April, crossing the River Po, and taking Bologna on the 21st and Verona on the 26th. A formal surrender took place on May 2. Mussolini, rescued from arrest by the Germans on September 12, 1943 and placed at the head of the puppet Italian Social Republic, was captured and shot by partisans on April 28.

ABOVE
US machine-gunners watch tanks and artillery firing on German positions around Monte Valbura, April 17.

RIGHT
8th Army attacked the River Senio on April 9, on the heels of a ferocious bombardment whose smoke shrouds the sky behind this tank. Its name suggests a Canadian origin, but the 1st Canadian Corps had left Italy for north-west Europe in March 1945.

ABOVE
The bodies of Mussolini and several
of his associates are exhibited in
Milan's Piazza Loreto. His mistress,
Clara Petacci, hangs alongside him.

Two young Germans captured by 52nd
(Lowland) Division at Hongen on January 20.

ALLIED ADVANCE INTO GERMANY

There was more bitter fighting as Montgomery cleared the
Reichswald and the Hochwald to close up on the Rhine in late
March. Further south, Hodges' 1st Army captured the bridge
at Remagen, between Bonn and Cologne, intact on March 7,
and on March 22 Patton's 3rd Army crossed the Rhine south
of Mainz. Montgomery staged his own crossing, on a grand scale,
on the night of 23–4 March. The two American armies closed round
the Ruhr pocket, taking over 400,000 prisoners, in early April.

LEFT
Overwhelming force: a German emerges from the rubble of Cleves, north-east of the Reichswald.

BELOW
The Ludendorff railway bridge over the Rhine at Remagen was captured on March 7, and five German officers were summarily shot for allowing it to be taken intact. This photograph show the bridge after it collapsed on the afternoon of March 17, after five US divisions had crossed.

LEFT

Montgomery's Rhine crossing, Operation *Plunder*, was covered by Operation *Varsity*, the dropping of two airborne divisions east of Wesel on the morning of March 24. In this photograph RAF Stirlings tow Horsa gliders over the Rhine.

BELOW

British troops crossing the Rhine.

ABOVE
The strain of captivity is etched
deep into the faces of these British
prisoners of war, liberated by the
Americans at Göttingen on April 8.

British prisoners of war greet the liberators of Stalag 11B, near Fallingbostel.

RIGHT

Montgomery reads regional surrender terms to the German delegation on Lüneburg Heath, May 4. There were total surrenders at Rheims and at Karlshorst, on the eastern edge of Berlin.

RIGHT
Many Germans committed suicide rather than surrender. Here the mayor of Leipzig is slumped over his desk, with his wife in an armchair and his daughter, in a nurse's uniform, on the settee, April 25.

BELOW
This deeply symbolic shot, taken after American capture of Nuremberg on April 20, shows a knocked-out Sherman in front of the tiers of empty seats in the stadium which once echoed the applause for Hitler. Contrast it with the picture on page 16.

THE PACIFIC WAR

American B-29s based in the Marianas began bombing Japan in November 1944. The tiny island of Iwo Jima, between the Marianas and Tokyo, and thus an invaluable base for the strategic air offensive, was attacked in February 1945 but took almost a month to clear. Okinawa was invaded on April 1, and the Japanese fought fiercely for its interior organized resistance ceased only on June 21. With Okinawa in their hands, the Americans were in a position to close in on the Japanese home islands, though it was not a prospect many relished.

RIGHT

When the American entered Manila, capital of the Philippines, on February 4, they found these US civilians in Santo Tomas University, used as a Japanese internment camp.

BELOW

US Marines on the beach at Iwo Jima, February 19, with Mount Suribachi rising in the background. It took the Marines 36 days and over 23,000 casualties to take the island: only 216 of the garrison of 20,000 were captured.

OPPOSITE PAGE

Raising the flag on Mount Suribachi. This, one of the most famous war photographs ever taken is posed: a smaller flag had been raised two hours earlier.

The oldest carrier in American service, the
USS *Saratoga* was hit on February 21, off Iwo
Jima, but managed to make her way back
to Puget Navy Yard on the US Pacific coast.

During operations against Kyushu in
March USS *Franklin* was badly damaged
by air attack. Her crew suffered about
1,000 casualties, but she was saved by
the determination of her crew and the
US Navy's emphasis on damage control,
and limped back to Brooklyn Navy
Yard under her own power.

Rockets from a US Navy landing craft
streak ashore in support of an Australian
landing on the oil-rich island of Tarakan,
off the east coast of Borneo, April 30.

ABOVE

Off Ie Shima, a tiny island in the Ryuku
archipelago, an American battleship fires a
barrage at a Japanese aircraft: it is almost
hidden by smoke and spray, just above the
horizon and slightly left of centre.

Japanese kamikaze pilots deliberately
crashed their aircraft into enemy
warships: the practice became official
policy in October 1944. Kamikaze attacks
reached their zenith during the battle for
Okinawa: here a kamikaze pilot narrowly
misses the battleship USS *Missouri*.

An American battleship blasts Okinawa
as a line of Amtracks heads for the beach.

RIGHT
A flame-thrower tank clearing
Japanese snipers from caves on Okinawa.

The newly-formed British Pacific Fleet joined the Americans in March. This photograph show wreckage being cleared off the carrier HMS *Formidable* after a kamikaze attack, May 4.

This aerial view of the industrial area of Tokyo, taken after the war, shows the effect of American bombing.

BURMA AND THE FAR EAST

In Burma, 14th Army crossed the Chindwin in December 1944 and advanced on the Irrawaddy. In a deft flanking manoeuvre Slim crossed the river south of Mandalay and took the communication centre of Meitktila, beating off a fierce counterattack: Mandalay itself fell on March 20. The way to Rangoon was now open, and the city was taken by an amphibious attack, Operation *Dracula*. Encircled Japanese from the Arakan tried to break out south-eastwards without success, and sporadic fighting east of the Sittang ended after the Japanese surrender.

ABOVE
A British 3-inch mortar in action during the fighting for Meiktila.

LEFT

The battle of the last ten yards: Sikhs rush a Japanese position still smoking from phosphorous grenades.

BELOW

During the advance down the Arakan a Garhwali (an Indian soldier often confused with a Gurkha), covered by a rifleman on his left, throws a phosphorous grenade.

British and Indian paratroops were dropped near Rangoon on May 1 and an amphibious force moved up the Rangoon river to take the Burmese capital on the May 3.

RIGHT
A Japanese private carrying a white flag at Abya on the Sittang during mopping-up operations, August 30

The price of victory: men of 4th Battalion, The Royal West Kents, visit the graves of their comrades at Kohima.

RIGHT

Far East prisoners of war, given the bare minimum of food and shelter, were often worked hard and were subject to frequent brutal assault, in part because of the Japanese conviction that surrender was disgraceful. These prisoners were liberated in Rangoon.

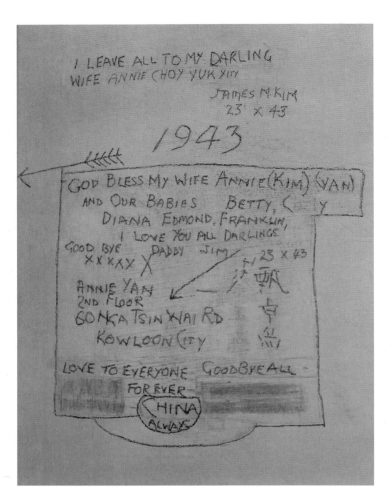

LEFT
James M. Kim, a Chinese member of the Hong Kong Defence Force, left this poignant last testament on the wall of his cell in Stanley Prison before his execution in 1943.

RIGHT
A month after her liberation, British internee Wendy Rossini shows the daily ration of rice and stew given to all five occupants of her room in Stanley Camp, Hong Kong.

YALTA AND POTSDAM

Allied strategy evolved at twelve major conferences, beginning at Placentia Bay before US entry into the war and going on to Potsdam, after the end of the European war. Churchill, Roosevelt and Stalin held their summit at Yalta in February 1945, where the organization of the postwar world was the major topic of discussion. It was the last time the "big three" met, for by the time of the Potsdam conference in July and August Roosevelt was dead. Churchill, who lost that summer's general election, handed over to Clement Attlee during the conference.

The big three at Yalta. They agreed that Germany should be divided, and that the borders of Poland should be moved westwards.

Winston Churchill and new US
President Harry Truman at Potsdam.

Truman is flanked at Potsdam by Stalin
and a smiling Clement Attlee, the
new British Labour Prime Minister.
The conference marked the break-up
of the wartime alliance and the start of the
nuclear age, for it was there that Truman
told Stalin of the atomic bomb's existence.

DRESDEN

During 1944 the Americans established growing air superiority over Germany as the Luftwaffe's fighters lost ever more heavily in battles against the fighters escorting US bomber formations. This in turn helped take pressure off the RAF's increasingly accurate night attacks, and by 1945 the combined bomber offensive rolled on with unprecedented destructive power. Bombing devastated the German transport system, produced severe fuel shortages, and levelled most major towns. It eventually crippled the German economy, although this task proved far more difficult and costly than most advocates of strategic bombing had ever imagined.

BELOW

The USAAF followed up with a daylight raid. Much of Dresden was razed, and perhaps 50,000 people were killed. Churchill felt that the raid "remains a serious query against the conduct of Allied bombing." Harris, however, declared that the remaining cities of Germany were "not worth the bones of one British Grenadier."

ABOVE

The beautiful city of Dresden, capital of Saxony, was not seriously bombed till February 1945, when the Allies attacked it as part of a plan to add to chaos in Germany and demonstrate, at the imminent Yalta conference, that they were supporting the Russian offensive. Here a firestorm rages during the RAF's night attack.

Troops of the British 6th Airborne
Division (including, third from right,
Private R.C. Sutherland of 1st Canadian
Parachute Battalion) meet Russians near
Wismar, on the Baltic coast, on May 3.

ALLIED–SOVIET LINK UP

Given the rapidity with which the iron curtain was to descend across
Europe it was easy to forget how great was the popular regard
for the Russians in much of the West. Although these photographs
of the meetings between the Russians and the Western Allies
deliver a propaganda message, they also reflect genuine emotions.

Russians and Americans meet at
Torgau on the Elbe on the afternoon
on April 25. Here a Russian major
enjoys a cigarette with his allies.

Not only is Eisenhower in mellow mood at this first meeting of the Allied Control Commission in Berlin in June, but even Montgomery, in conversation with Zhukov, seems unusually relaxed.

The 22-year-old Feodora Bondenko controlling traffic at Berlin's Brandenburg Gate, July 5.

Bomb damage in Hiroshima looking toward the hypocentre. To date the bomb has killed, by blast and flash at the time or by radiation subsequently, perhaps 140,000 people. Survivors have suffered a variety of illness and mental trauma.

The mushroom cloud over Nagasaki. Although "Fat Man" was a more powerful weapon than "Little Boy", the topography of Nagasaki meant that it inflicted less damage. About 75,000 people were killed and as many again injured.

The A-bombs brought quick acceptance of terms that, wisely, left the Emperor Hirohito on the throne. The formal surrender was signed aboard USS *Missouri*, in Tokyo Bay on 2 September. Behind MacArthur stand Wainwright and Percival, the defeated commanders of 1942.

HIROSHIMA AND NAGASAKI

The Manhattan Project combined British and American scientists in the research that led to the testing of the first atomic bomb near Alamogordo, New Mexico, in July 1945. Although the bomb was first conceived as a response to similar German work, by 1945 it was seen as both a way of ending the war against Japan and applying pressure to the Russians. The first atomic bomb to be used militarily, "Little Boy", was dropped on Hiroshima on August 6 from a B29 bomber based on the Pacific island of Tinian. Another Tinian-based bomber dropped the second, "Fat Man", on Nagasaki, on August 9.

THE END OF THE WAR

There were two distinct victory celebrations, the first on VE (Victory in Europe) Day on May 8, and the second on VJ (Victory over Japan) Day on August 15. Given the narrow margin of Britain's survival in 1940 and the legacy of the First World War there was particular sense of gratitude in Britain on VE Day. However, those still fighting in the Pacific were struck by the irony that they continued to risk their lives. For them, and for most Americans, the deeper relief came on VJ Day.

PRECEDING PAGE
VE Day celebrations in London outside the American Red Cross "Rainbow Corner".

BELOW
Churchill is mobbed by crowds in Whitehall after making his triumphant VE Day speech to the House of Commons.

ABOVE
American soldiers, with a little local help, parade the Stars and Stripes across Piccadilly Circus on VJ Day.

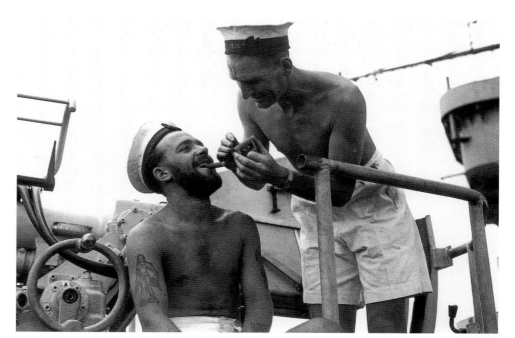

RIGHT
Leading Seaman Alfred Dennis of Plymouth, a veteran of the Arctic convoys and the *Torch* Landings, enjoys VJ Day aboard HMS *Shah* in the Far East and allows himself to think of life beyond 1945.

INDEX

PICTURE CREDITS

All the photographs reproduced in the book have been taken from the collections of the Photograph Archive at the Imperial War Museum. The Museum's reference numbers for each of the photographs are listed below, giving the page on which they appear in the book and any location indicator (t –top, b –bottom, l –left, r –right, c –centre)

10	HU5517	70b	HU1147	138	HU71891	206	E18523	278	K5287	340	EA35413
14	NYP68046	71t	H1619	139r	D63768	207	E19129	279	NA6630	341	HU66477
15	FRA204717	71b	H1635	139l	TR86	208	E19353	280	NA6813	342t	NYF35224
16	HU18257	72	HU2286	140	H18068	209	CBM1833	281	NA7136	342b	EA33708
17	MH13118	73t	COL291	141t	CM645	210	MH 4981	282t	HU 55080	343t	K7586
18	HU47654	73b	COL293	141b	K325	211t	D18488	282b	NA7414	343b	BU1163
19t	HU32986	74	HU75880	142t	MH23643	211b	D4852	283t	NA7748	344t	BU1126
19b	HU34723	76t	HU49148	142b	BM2252	212t	D18506	283b	NA9162	344b	MH3956
20	HU39750	76b	MH1926	143t	HU381	212b	D18512	284t	NA9299	345t	BU1122
21t	CHN260	77	MH9411	143b	MH15931	213t	CH5712	284b	NA10208	345b	EA38134
21b	CHN316	78	HU2283	144	ZZZ3130C	213b	HU57227	287	RUS4324	346	EA48015
22	HU3902	79	HU3002	145t	N396	214t	HU36275	286r	RR1885	347	EA47958
23t	HU50097	80	HU3266	145b	NA676	214b	HU54542	286b	RUS4409	348t	EA48337
23b	HU4255	81	HU3616	146	HU39586	215	A9115	287	MH12868	348b	FRA200193
24t	D8193	82t	H3277	147t	HU39577	216	HU36192	288t	HU60392	349	EA68789
24b	HU5489	82b	HU76027	147b	MH 9245	217	TR464	288b	RUS4403	350l	CH16280
25	MH13154	83t	HU68019	148	HU39614	218	A11231	289	HU55631	350r	CL3407
26	HU5481	83b	HU63611	149	HU39661	219t	HU1808	290	A7549	351	D21213
27	HU75345	84	HU49250	150t	HU39630	219b	HU1890	291	A21167	352	HU36227
28	HU5551	85	LN6194	150b	HU39578	220	HU22580	292-3	A21202	353t	HU86187
29	MH24390	86t	D2040	151t	HU5065	221t	NY13825	298t	IA15552	353b	HU44874
30	HU5517	86c	HU36228	151b	HU39619	221b	MH9053	298b	EA17886	354t	CEM1014
31t	HU5532	86b	HU36121	152-3	HU5063	222t	15964	299t	NA12900	354b	TR1783
31b	HU5533	87t	D734	154t	RUS1263	222b	GM1480	299b	MH1984	355t	PD270
32t	HU5547	87b	D1218	154b	FRA101562	223	A11180	300	NA4848	355b	OEM83
32b	HU36530	88-9	A726	155t	FLM724	224	CH5466	301	TR1799	356t	MH2111B
33	HU5490	90	C1785	155b	RUS1206	225	HU40173	302t	TR1797	356b	TR1386
34t	MH13130	91t	C1781	156-7	RUS1266	226	C2564	302c	TR1800	357t	RUS600
34b	HU5520	91b	C826	158	HU3525	227	C3186	302b	TR1802	357b	NYP11839
35t	HU75349	92t	H1594	159	MISC54424	228t	C3268	303	HU55161	362t	RUS5138
35b	HU5505	92c	HU55535	160	NYF 22545	228b	HU8237	304t	NA11406	362b	RR2322
36t	HU5455	92b	H2554	161t	OEM21469	229	C3295	304b	MH6366	363t	RR2333
36c	MH13135	93	H2005	161b	MH6014	230	A12661	305t	NA15295	363b	HU68178
36b	MH13127	94t	HU7652	162t	OEM21470	231	A12835	305b	NA15534	364t	NYP36236
267	HU5524	94b	CH15173	162b	HU56120	236	NA1008	306t	NA15520	364b	BU3743
268	D648	95	CH15332	163	K1325	237t	NA1096	306b	HU55349	365t	EA65160
39t	HU5476	96t	C1869	164-5	K1367	237b	NA1043	307t	NYP27322	365b	EA62972
39b	HU5516	96b	CH1269	166t	HU2780	238t	NY5815	307b	NYF39284	366t	IA63699
40t	HU86051	97t	CH1522	166b	HU39405	238b	NY6460	308	HU55113	366b	NA2383
40b	HU55665	97b	H4725	167t	FE352	239t	C3225	309t	CF175	367	HU50242
41t	HU86049	98-9	HU1062	167b	HU86173	239b	A20687	309b	MH7237	368	B13905
41b	HU86048	100t	CH192	168t	K4025	240t	TR100	310	IND2290	369t	B14609
42t	O1	100b	HU3093	168b	HU2473	240b	A14892	311	IB283	369b	EA58495
42b	O86	101	C5422	169	HU2675	247	CAN2074	312t	IND3263	370t	CL2232
43t	O308	102	HU23746	174t	K758	242	FLM1461	312b	IND3285	370b	BU2167
43b	O2142	103t	C2416	174b	FLM908	243t	CAN/A4059	313t	IND2994	371	EA61489A
44-5	A6	103b	HU3121	175	HU31329	243c	HU40194	313c	IND2653	372t	BU3661
46	HU5519	104	MH2718	176	HU2769	243b	C4292	313b	IND3702	372b	BU5207
47	HU55569	105t	H3514	177	K974	244	C3543	314t	EA21088	373t	EA63953
48	CH192	105b	H5597	178t	JAR1240	245	ZZZ11988F	314b	NYF50015	373b	EA63545
52	HU5206	106	ZZZ3928E	178b	K2204	246	NA3433	315t	IND3766	374t	NYP58366
53t	NYP68074	107	D1516	179	HU2772	247t	HU74967	315b	SE1884	374b	HU3344
53b	A42	108	HU65956	180t	NAP246225	247b	HU74965	316t	NYP30679	375	NYP59700
54	HU55639	109t	D1091	180b	NYP60749	248	AUS1615	316b	AP73239	376	NYF74296
55t	HU86050	109b	HU1176	181	HU61323	250	MH1051	317t	AP38269	377t	NYP80747
55b	N181	110t	MH3802	182	HU2764	251	OEM4356	317b	PLP775F	377b	NYF69518
56-57	STT914	110b	E1495	183t	OEM1566	251t	MH9260	318t	PL12815E	378	HU3069
58t	HU2873	111t	E839	183b	OEM 22403	251b	MH6255	318b	KY8495F	381	NYF70679
58b	MH2619	111b	E1426	184	AP61595	252t	NYF14359	319t	HU31075	380t	MH24367
59	O190	116	E1553	185	NYF 42432	252b	ZZZ7290E	319b	HU86081	380b	NYP68819
60	F4341	117	E1579	186	RUS1124	253	ZZZ11408E	320t	MH4491	381t	MH21119
61t	HU31493	118t	CM354	187t	HU40176	254	EN10800	320b	MH4489	381b	KY49605
61b	MH9214	118b	E1766	187b	MISC60746	255	NYP11545	324	NYP30649	382	SE3281
62t	PC449	119t	MH5559	188t	RUS1371	256	CH18005	325	NYF31168	383t	IND4550
62b	MH9417	119b	A9801	188b	HU40285	257t	HU69915	323t	NUYF18668	383b	IND4175
63t	HU3789	120t	RML650	189	HU40302	257b	HU4594	323b	KY483471	384t	CI1296
63b	STT848	120b	E2885	190t	HU5152	258	TR1125	324	NYF33919	384b	SE4610
64t	F461OF	121t	HU1205	190b	HU5140	259t	A14149	325t	NYF57021	385t	IND4882
64b	HU49122	121b	RML596	191t	HU5138	259b	E26634	325b	NYF47538	385b	SE3991
65t	HU3794	122t	MH5588	191b	RUS3699	260t	NA4183	326	CP51763	386t	A30559
65b	F4483F	122b	HU5628	192t	HU68994	260b	NY605	327t	EA25511	386b	A30549
66	F4424	123t	MH5591	192b	MH9704	261	TA18	327b	MH2076	387	NAM237
67t	HU57681	123b	E6751	193t	MH9701	262-3	GL885	330	EA25902	388t	TR2920
67b	HU55640	124	AX24A	193b	RUS3760	264t	NA5388	329t	AP25726	388b	BU9496
68t	HU28992	126t	HU39471	194t	CBM1583	264b	NYF9892	329b	MH4505	389t	C4972
68b	HU2280	126b	HU39517	194b	TR1	265l	TR1246	330t	B5114	389b	HU44924
69	H1628	127t	HU39524	195	E3959E	265r	TR1240	330b	MH2408	390t	BU5230
70t	HU1145	127b	HU39512	196t	IND885	266t	TR1252	331	EA26941	390b	OWIL64545
		128	E3021E	196b	E12919	266b	TR1250	332	B5968	391t	FRA204091
		129	A4154	197t	E12789	269	HU3023	333	B5382	391b	HU86189
		130	HU55013	197b	MH5854	268	TR1156	334t	KY30558	392	MH2629
		131	HU39540	198t	MH5856	269	CH11641	334b	B6618	393t	MH2649
		132	A4815	198b	E12870	274	C3371	335t	B5667	393b	A30426
		133t	E2993	199t	HU40255	271	HU44474	335b	MH9097	394-5	EA65797
		133b	BM5392	199b	E13940	272-3	NYF14138	336	EA31701	396	HU6188
		134-135	HU2430	200-1	E15560	274	NYP21768A	337t	EA33756	397t	EA75894
		136t	HU68753	202	MH5843	275	AP261026	337b	EA29765	397b	A30199
		136b	BM3855	203	E18465	276t	HU42331	338t	EA33763		
		137t	BM4457	204	E18511	276b	MH13407	338b	MH11151		
		137b	AUS704	205	E18493	277	HU12143	339	OWIL35108		